The Shortest Distance between Two Points Is Not a Straight Line in Africa

Real Life Stories from the Front Line while Doing Business on the Continent

Ben Konate

Published in Switzerland 2018

e-book ISBN 978 2 9701244 1 2

Paperback ISBN 978 2 9701244 0 5

For Marie-Laure, Yanis and Maurice,

Introduction

The idea of this book comes from a very simple observation: Despite my 20-plus years of experience doing business in Africa, from Casablanca to Johannesburg, from Dakar to Nairobi, the depth of my knowledge on doing business in Africa remains nanoscopic. I indeed spent decades of my professional life roaming the continent in various capacities and in different industries, but I am still far from asserting, "I know how to do business in Africa." However, if I believe that it would take a person more than one lifetime to grasp the intricacies of doing business in Africa, it takes the aggregate of many people's life experiences to get a PhD in the field. With the understanding that I may not be a full-fledged expert on doing business in Africa, I set out to develop strong bonds and close friendships with a large number of people who assuredly do know Africa, and how to do business in Africa (or more precisely, in their particular industries and in specific parts of Africa). Every time I get a chance to sit with one of them, I always marvel at their experience and practical knowledge, and at how untapped and sparse this knowledge base is. I therefore set out to consolidate this knowledge in a book.

I chose the title, *The Shortest Distance between Two Points Is Not a Straight Line in Africa*, to illustrate the commonly shared view among people with experience in doing business in Africa that more often than not, simple matters prove to be intrinsically more complicated than they look, and matters that appear seemingly complicated are even more Daedalean than imagined. Daedalean, but not impossible, for they require a different paradigm, not the usual, textbook approach to addressing business concerns practiced in Western contexts (or in any other contexts for that matter, i.e., Asian, South American, etc.).

The seeming inanity in the title perfectly captures my idea that more often than not in Africa, the obvious shortcut is certainly harder—if not impossible—to cross, for reasons that are not apparent in the first place. This is far from saying that solutions do not exist, but there is always more than meets the eyes to reach them and to make a long-term success of a business enterprise.

Mathematically speaking, there is a case demonstrating that "the shortest distance between two points is indeed the straight line" as Archimedes reportedly enunciated first.[1] The demonstration of this geometric postulate involves uses of derivatives, integrals, and the Euler–Lagrange equation, but as it appears, this is true only in Euclidean space (a flat surface). In non-Euclidean spaces (i.e.,

---

[1] Archimedes of Syracuse, Greek mathematician c. 287 – c. 212 BC

spheres or other shapes), the shortest distance between two points *not* being a straight line is also a possibility. We think of the shortest distance between two points as being a straight line because of our basic human tendency to oversimplify. Africa—as many other places, I imagine—should particularly be considered a non-Euclidean universe when it comes to business.

I am wholeheartedly passionate about business and about Africa. I have the fervent conviction that creating a fertile business environment and a business-savvy generation of entrepreneurs and leaders in Africa is one of the best ways to pull the continent resolutely on the path of emergence. It would surely take more than that alone to achieve the goal of counting Africa among the developed nations, but raising the bar when it comes to our expertise in doing business and generating economic prosperity is without doubt one of the best ways that I know of to move the needle in terms of the welfare of populations in Africa and of lifting the continent up.

My approach in this book is inspired by our African storytelling culture. I recount real-life experiences for the reader to learn from, in the form of anecdotes and in a style that is easy to read, fun, and insightful.

The concept of the wisdom of crowds proves

rewarding in discussing doing business in Africa.[1] The book is organized in a free-flow format, and provides a series of anecdotes detailing the particular story of a project, business endeavor, or concept from which the main protagonists drew a deep insight, which could benefit the reader. I tried to include as many details as possible from the cases and the real names of the people involved whenever I was given permission to do so. I have on two occasions only changed the names of the organizations, projects, products, or people in the book in an effort to conceal the identities of the contributors and the companies they were discussing due to privacy or confidentiality concerns, and tried at the same time to maintain the full integrity of the story. I still narrated the facts as they happened for the reader to get the gist of the case. Except for these two instances, all the stories, facts, dates, names, and locations are real and unaltered, as recounted by the contributors. The contributors are all professionals with a profound knowledge of Africa and an international business exposure, which allows us to draw parallels between their experiences in emerging markets and developed markets.

I initially considered including drawings, but changed my mind several times as people I consulted with regarding

---

[1] The Wisdom of Crowds: Why the Many Are Smarter Than the Few and How Collective Wisdom Shapes Business, Economies, Societies and Nations, 2004 - James Surowiecki

this book believed illustrations could take away from the seriousness of the work. Ultimately, I stuck with my original idea, essentially because it fits particularly well with the storytelling framework of the book.

I would like to thank all the contributors who enthusiastically accepted to join this project and share their successes, failures, experiences, advice, and stories of their lives while they were trying to make an impact in a challenging African market and to devise answers to some of the hardest business questions they ever faced.

Ben Konate

Chavannes-de-Bogis, Switzerland – April 2018

Table of Contents

Chapter I

Hamdallaye and the Answered Prayer

The makeshift football hit Abdoulaye on the shin, hard enough to pull him out of his daydream. An 11-year-old kid ran towards him to retrieve the ball so he could rejoin his classmates waiting to continue their football game. This is when the noise hit him. As if someone had suddenly turned up the volume, Abdoulaye noticed the commotion in the schoolyard, as hundreds of kids aged two to 18 played, yelled, ran, jumped, and engaged in all kinds of activities they could exercise during their 30-minute break between morning classes. The kid with the ball stopped in front of the towering figure of a man, intimidated and not really sure whether he should pick his ball up or go back without it. Abdoulaye smiled, bent to collect the ball, and handed it over to the child, whose name was Hamdi, a fifth-grade student. The kid fumbled some excuses in perfect French—*Excusez-moi Monsieur le Directeur*—and took off towards his friends. Abdoulaye was not the school director, but he was the founder of the institution, and the children respectfully used the term Monsieur when they addressed him. As he watched Hamdi leave, he remembered how long and tortuous his journey had been. A tear escaped his eye.

Abdoulaye Wann never intended to create a school of any scale. He merely set out to solve a growing problem for his own kids, and then for his friends' and other people's kids. The demand for quality education in Conakry, Guinea, at the time was enormous. The year was 1989, and it had only been about 5 years since the military took power in a bloodless coup d'état after the death of Ahmed Sékou Touré, the country's long-serving president. Before colonization and long before the international headlines of the Ebola outbreak in March 2014, the country had been home to famous West African empires, kingdoms, and epic battles.

In 1958, when then French President Charles de Gaulle offered West African colonies the choice between full independence or continuing their status with additional autonomy in a community of

states, Guinea was the only country to opt for its full independence. There was a catch, though: Any country choosing full independence would be cut off from any financial, economic, or technical aid from France. As history showed, the choice proved to be a capital mistake and a major political miscalculation. Sékou Touré's Guinea took the socialist direction, turning to countries such as China and Russia for support, and over time, he transitioned the country into a dictatorial regime. Economically, Guinea went to the bottom of the list and was classified at the time as one of the poorest in Africa. In 1990, according to the World Bank, Guinea was ranked 137 over 150 nations worldwide in terms of GDP per capita, based on purchasing power parity (PPP). The country's infrastructure, health system, public services, education, and economy were in shambles.

The year 1984 marked a significant turn for the 12 million people in the country as it progressively opened to a market-driven economy and enjoyed more liberties, such as holding democratic elections in 2010. IFIs (International Financial Institutions) such as the World Bank, IFC, IMF, IFAD, AfDB, and Foreign Direct Investments started paying a growing interest in the country and initiated projects that allowed for growth in the private sector. That year, while Guinea was sitting on shifting tectonic plates and about to see major changes coming its way after two and a half decades of dictatorial rule and economic lethargy, Indira Gandhi was assassinated by her Sikh security guards, Virgin Atlantic made its inaugural flight, the world witnessed the beginning of a widespread famine in Ethiopia, and Dr. Luc Montagnier, Robert Gallo, Jay Levy, and their teams of researchers announced the discovery of the AIDS virus. Also in 1984, Abdoulaye was quietly running a private transport in Conakry, the capital city of Guinea.

The "Failed" Businessman

Abdoulaye's transport company was actually a 450 square meter garage, which he had turned into a site for his transport operations. The garage was not far away from the Catholic nursery school John-Paul II. The school was an Italian, cooperation-funded project with its own community health center and a kindergarten with an education system in accordance with worldwide standards where kids enjoyed wide spaces for play as well as a strong curriculum. Such a school was very rare in Guinea at the time, and most parents from the expat community enrolled their children there.

Like many parents in Africa, Abdoulaye considered education to be the most important legacy he could leave his children. And only the best would do, no matter what it took.

"There was still a major issue," he tells me. "The institution had no primary school, and older kids or those completing kindergarten had to go to a different school to carry on with their education. Most of the parents, including me, had to drop off our kids at the kindergarten and then take a long trip across town to drop off the older kids at primary school before reaching our offices. It was a running challenge, and I often wondered how it could be solved. The idea of using my garage to build a primary school had been brewing in my mind for some time already, as my transport business was struggling. The idea stayed with me over the years and soon took on a life of its own. Because my garage was adjacent to the kindergarten, it was the perfect location for a primary school, which was, at the time, in great demand."

The transport company had indeed been on life support for quite a while and had finally run aground. Facing bankruptcy, the company began the winding-down process. During the final weeks before the company's liquidation, he made up his mind: he would turn the garage into a primary school and find a way to provide the primary education that his three children—a daughter, a son, and a nephew—deserved. A few of his friends quickly bought into his idea and entrusted their children with him as well. Soon enough, Abdoulaye, sitting on the ruins of a bankrupt transport company, found himself with the great responsibility of providing primary education to 11 children.

The Throes and Woes of Project Financing in Africa

Abdoulaye needed preliminary funding to turn the site into a real primary school. His initial thought was to partner with a few people who could help come up with the money to fund the project. However, this turned out to be a major hurdle. With the bankruptcy and closure of his transport company in the rearview mirror, Abdoulaye's lending credibility for a business was quite low.

"My reputation, as far as business ventures were concerned, had slumped when my transport company went bust. Everyone, including close friends, held silent doubts about my ability to start and run another business venture. In fact, many of them decided not to tide me over. They didn't have the facts about why I had to close shop. My ego took a serious hit. But I was determined to pull myself together and keep going. As we say in Africa, it is not what you are called, but what you answer to. I am a businessman, and failing is an inherent part of the game. This was a learning experience. I needed to turn the page and start a new chapter."

Most of the people he'd targeted as potential investors were shrewd traders, local loan sharks, and even a few friends and former business associates. Those kinds of investors were mostly looking for investments that could turn a profit in a couple of months. Abdoulaye discovered, with a pinch of consternation, that many of them expected their money back within a month or two, three maximum, and with decent returns, which mostly meant obscene interest rates. The nature of his project, a long-term and socially impactful venture, was therefore unattractive to those kinds of investors. It did not matter that a good number of them were personal friends, relatives, and former business associates. He changed tactics and took aim at commercial banks.

The year was 1991–92, and the two banks in question were the Moroccan Bank, Banque Populaire Maroco-Guinéenne, and UIBG (Union Internationale de Banque en Guinée), a subsidiary of the large French banking conglomerate, Crédit Lyonnais.[1] It was the largest bank at the time and was primarily state-owned. Abdoulaye was interested in a 5-year loan, and he took his first shot at the

---

[1] UIBG is today ORABANK in Guinea

Moroccan Bank. The manager was incredibly enthusiastic about his project. He knew too well about the challenges and misgivings of the educational sector in Guinea and was therefore sold on Abdoulaye's idea.

Unfortunately, the bank's last word on critical decisions, including loan approvals, did not lie with him. He informed a woebegone-looking Abdoulaye one afternoon when he had called on him as a follow-up, that his project was "unattractive to the bank and that it did not qualify as the kind of investments that the bank was looking to finance." Admittedly, Abdoulaye wasn't focusing on profits for the first 3 to 4 years, which was a deal breaker for the bank.

"If they were to give me the funds, apart from setting up the basic facilities, I would have immediately used the money to build a stable and strong image for the school and create a good name or reputation. Therefore, the project

seemed like a social project at the beginning, especially viewed from the bottom-line angle, which the bank was focused on. The considerations or signs of return on investment were not easily perceivable at the beginning or clear for the bank."

Six months later, and when discussions had all but floundered, Abdoulaye moved to the second bank, UIBG. He opened a bank account for the purpose of the loan, but he encountered the same frustration all over again.

He had lost a significant amount of time discussing the project with the banks, trying to secure funding. Two school years had gone by without any child being enrolled in his new school project. Although desperate for funding, Abdoulaye knew he could not wait any longer and that he had to roll out the project's operations with the meager financial means he had available. Therefore, he started his school in the rundown premises previously used as the base of his transport operations.

First Day of School

In September of 1994, almost 2 years after commencing funding negotiations with the banks, 37 kids showed up for their first day of class at his primary school. Abdoulaye worked in the school for 1 year and with only four teachers. One of the teachers also doubled as a director. Abdoulaye recalls that he practically ran the school's first year from his own pocket. The school was running on fumes, and his wife had to liquidate her clothing and sewing business to support him.

"My wife ran a fairly successful clothing and sewing business at the time, which she sold in order to support me financially with the school project. She also took up a great deal of the non-teaching roles, which included acting as cleaning lady of the school and making sure all the logistics ran smoothly."

The Bright Kid

As the school opened its doors for the second year, Abdoulaye received a rare call from one of his old mates from university who had encountered one of the pupils from his school. His friend was struck by the pupil's level of articulation in French.

"Abdoulaye, how is it going, my friend?" Moussa brawled in excitement before Abdoulaye could say hello.

"Everything is going quite well, Moussa. Many years it has been, my friend," Abdoulaye returned with equal enthusiasm.

"I have an excellent kid here with me, quite articulate and speaking fine French. His name is Ibrahima, and he says that he goes to your school."

"Is that so?" said Abdoulaye, thrown by the subtle compliment. "Why, yes, I started up a school, and it is now in its second year," he beamed.

Moussa was taken aback by the level of French the pupil could command and by his overall grasp and articulation of the French language, as this was uncommon in the country. French was the official language but still not widely and properly used, and it was often that pupils spoke just a few words of French, heavily mixed with one of the local languages, such as Susu, Malinké, Pular, or Kissi, just to name the more common ones. He knew at once that it had to be the result of an excellent teaching institution and was stirred when he learnt that it was actually a school owned by his old classmate from university. Moussa would call on him a couple of days later, interested in the project and in how Abdoulaye had already kick-started it without any external funding. At the time, Moussa worked for an organization called OPIP (Office de Promotion des Investissements

Privés), a government development assistance organization that fell under the Ministry of Commerce and Industry. OPIP was primarily concerned with the promotion of local investment initiatives. It was a joint initiative put in place by the government and the United Nations Industrial Development Organization (UNIDO), and was funded through a local bank, BICIGUI (Banque Internationale pour le Commerce et l'Industrie de Guinée).

The main aim of OPIP was to help the government transition the country from a socialist economy to a more liberal economy. The basic idea was to grow the private sector by supporting private ventures. Abdoulaye recalls that during Sékou Touré times, all the university graduates were guaranteed a job at the various government ministries. But this became a problem over time as all the available positions filled up. The new government then faced pressure to grow the private sector so that it could absorb the graduates and the growing number of unemployed youths. The UN had stepped in to alleviate this problem, leading to the formation of OPIP. Moussa helped to get Abdoulaye's school into the list of projects that would be funded by OPIP.

"Moussa really assisted me in getting through the ropes and securing some funding from OPIP. The funds were much less than what we needed, owing to the total number of projects that had also lined up to receive funding from OPIP. The available funds had to be shared out. Another point that was critical for us was that this helped us become known to BICIGUI."

Abdoulaye's school received the equivalent of US$50,000 in funding that year. The organization happened to be looking for such projects and was happy to release a second round of financing to the successful projects. Because of the school's remarkable performance and more apparent growth prospects, Abdoulaye received a second round of financing. Many of the projects that had received the initial round of financing actually failed.

Government Support

Despite the fact that education has a social objective and that governments are key stakeholders, the Minister of Education at the time had, quite rightly, surmised that educating the children in the country could not be achieved without involving the private sector. Mrs. Aïcha Bah Diallo, the then Minister of Pre-University Education and Vocational Training, had set up an entire department within the ministry dedicated to the private education sector. The department set about making all the facilities, accreditations, licences, and requirements easily accessible to the private sector.

At this moment, I clearly notice the rise in Abdoulaye's voice, which betrays the genuine emotions he feels when he mentions Mrs. Diallo's name.

"Mrs. Aïcha Bah Diallo was an extraordinary woman, a true leader at the Ministry of Health. I was blessed that she happened to be in charge at the time. She studied chemistry in the US and had worked as a teacher and headmaster in Guinea. She was therefore familiar with the issue of education in the country. She had had a difficult life during the post-colonial regime. Her husband had been imprisoned, and she had to leave the country at some point, only to return when the regime changed. Her vision for the education system in Guinea set us on course to fulfil our own ambitions with our project."

The funding from OPIP and the new setup at the ministry helped Abdoulaye prepare for the new school year. He acquired a small school bus, built a sports field, and opened up a school canteen. The school bus was uniquely designed so that the kids could read books, recite poems, and carry out all kinds of games and singing activities within the bus.

"The kids were excited and happy to use the school

bus, which stood out among other school buses. The community took note, and soon more kids wanted to join our school, Hamdallaye. Enrolment shot up nearly 200%, with 118 children signing up the following year, from 37 children the first year. The school would then experience subsequent rapid growth in enrolments, approximately 100%, year after year."

Even in the midst of the exponential growth and expansion of the school, Abdoulaye was incredibly focused on delivering nothing short of quality education. He scouted educational materials from some of the best schools in neighbouring French-speaking countries such as Côte d'Ivoire and Mali and benchmarked his own curriculum.

"I studied nearly all the syllabi and education materials from other West African countries. I collected all the ideas and merged them into a unique curriculum that would not only suit the demand for my country's education programs, but would go beyond such demands."

Abdoulaye recalls that he directed the funds provided by OPIP towards development of the curriculum as well as the interiors of the classrooms. Apart from the sports field, the canteen, and the school bus, he did not really prioritize the external look of the school, certainly not in terms of budgetary allocation. He needed to rigorously manage the funding that he had received up to that point and wring out all the possible benefits in areas where they mattered most.

The World Bank Comes Knocking

In the first year, there were only four classes for each of the class years; First Grade (or CP1 in the French educational system, for Cours Préparatoire 1, for 6- to 7-year-old students), Second Grade (CP2, for Cours Préparatoire 2, for 6- to 7-year-old students), Third Grade (CE1, for Cours Elémentaire 1, for 7- to 8-year-old kids), and Fourth Grade (CE2, for Cours Elémentaire 2, for 8- to 9-year-old kids). With the kind of growth rates the school was experiencing, it would only be a matter of time before the kids would be heading to secondary school. Abdoulaye realized that this would be the next step on which he would focus his attention. A friend introduced him to an official at the World Bank who took keen interest in the project as soon as she heard about it. At the time (1997–98), the World Bank was looking for such projects to fund in the private sector.

Discussions began in earnest, and Abdoulaye was keen to secure funding from the World Bank to improve his primary school as well as to expand by adding a secondary school to the group. Interactions with the World Bank inadvertently opened a lot of doors for him, including those previously closed to him at the local commercial banks.

"Word quickly spread around that the World Bank was planning to fund the school. Other financiers and businesses were now more than willing to work with us and offer support. Whenever I needed a few bags of cement to build up something within the school, suppliers would line up to provide the goods even on credit. They already had imagined that a big bank was behind us and that money would not be a problem."

In the meantime, Abdoulaye was setting up the first secondary school class within the compound of the primary school while he embarked on building the secondary school. From a funding perspective, Hamdallaye School was a small venture for the World Bank. The size of the venture in terms of the investment required fell way below the minimum threshold. However, the potential impact of the project to the community, and perhaps Abdoulaye's unwavering commitment to the project, compelled the World Bank to remain interested.

This interest from the institution might have rubbed off onto some of the World Bank officials, according to Abdoulaye's recollection. A number of them would occasionally go out of their way to help push the project forward. Abdoulaye required a lot of help.

"It was a completely different ball game, especially compared to my earlier experiences with commercial banks. I had to adapt to the demands and requirements of the World Bank if I was going to get as much as a consideration."

The official he had been introduced to persuade the World Bank to look into the project and provide as much help as it could. The immediate issue then became how to work out the modalities that would allow the funds to reach the school. Other challenges would pop up with every small forward movement. The risk on the foreign exchange currency turned out to be higher than the risk on the interest rate.

"The local currency was devaluating quite fast in Guinea. The risk that we could not repay the loan because of the devaluation was actually higher than risk on the interest rate the bank was taking. It became the biggest hurdle up to that point. It was a complex hurdle, and I sunk in despair as soon as this information was relayed."

But the World Bank officials proposed an ingenious solution to the problem. They set up a guarantee mechanism with BICIGUI, the bank with which Abdoulaye had already developed a track record in terms of servicing the funds he got from OPIP. The World Bank would come in as a guarantor to the loan BICIGUI would make to the project, so the commercial bank would fund the school directly in local currency. If the currency situation deteriorated further, the project would be protected from the increasing burden of the debt by repaying its loan in Guinean francs. The World Bank exposure to loan default would be limited under that scenario, in terms of equivalent amount in hard currency the bank would have promised to cover for the project at the signature of the loan. The financial mechanism—local currency loans—is well oiled at the World Bank and is part of several financial tools the World Bank deploys in emerging markets to advance development through the private sector. The World Bank has made financing available to the private sector in more than 70 locally denominated currencies. The BICIGUI bank manager agreed, and a tripartite contract was signed between Abdoulaye, BICIGUI, and the World Bank.

Abdoulaye notes that while Hamdallaye School was one ambitious project, it had to be broken down into smaller subsections. The first tranche of the project's development required US\$200,000. With the World Bank's backing, the school received the first batch of funding from the local commercial bank. Since the World Bank guaranteed the loan and the interest, they required some kind of collateral—as would any other lender—from Abdoulaye. He had to sign off the mortgage on his property.

Interestingly, mortgage documents, or even property documentation as land title, never existed at the time in Guinea. Abdoulaye was once again in limbo. He had to approach the relevant departments—property surveyor, notary public, and property registry—and negotiate a title or any kind of legitimate documentation to show his ownership of the property. The World Bank understood the situation and agreed to wait for him to secure the documents, giving him a 10-month moratorium. One of the requirements by IFC was that a local lawyer would need to provide legal assurances in accordance with the national legislation. The lawyer was to certify that the deal was carried out within the confines of the law in Guinea. Abdoulaye had to find a lawyer who would then be required to meet up with the World Bank's legal advisor. As soon as the lawyer noticed that the deal involved the World Bank, he charged a premium fee for his services on the suspicion that a lot of money was involved.

"As soon as he saw that a big international financial institution had come into town to fund a project, he immediately thought he'd hit the jackpot. He thought he could finally land a big financial breakthrough and asked for exorbitant fees as a result. We were the ones to cover the legal fees and were now facing a huge legal bill. I went back to him and said, 'Look, how many more kids do I have to go and register back at the school so that I can afford to pay this bill? I don't think that this is reasonable.' I simply couldn't afford it, and it became a whole new hurdle for me."

When the haggling for the fees with the lawyer bore no fruit, the World Bank had to send in their legal advisor to Conakry for a second meeting. This time, top on the list of the agenda was to persuade the local lawyer to lower his fees and to prove to him that the project was not a money-minting exercise. The World Bank's legal advisor had to explain and confirm to the lawyer that Abdoulaye was the one footing the bill and that if the condition was not met, the school would not get the funding. The lawyer finally caved in and asked Abdoulaye how much he could pay before finally preparing the documentation and settling on an affordable fee for his services.

The project gained support from the parents as well. There was now an army of parents behind every step. A few influential parents would always try to assist whenever the school ran into administrative hurdles.

"Whenever there was a challenge or obstacle, one or two parents would step in and say, 'No, no, no, this is for our kids and it needs to move forward.' They would use their influence to help the school get past some of the hurdles that had to do with administration and regulation."

The entire process took a whole year to complete, and the funds were finally released to the school. Abdoulaye concedes that he took a huge gamble. He set his sights on beginning the New Year with a secondary school in place. Therefore, he had secured a collection of short and small loans to help set up the secondary school even as he anticipated closing the funding deal with the World Bank. There were virtually no guarantees from the financial institution, and the entire process seemed ready to collapse or face a new hurdle with each passing month. Perhaps moved by his vision and passion, Abdoulaye went ahead and set up the secondary school anyway, determined on having the first batch of first-year students enrolled in the new school.

The World Bank's commitment and dedication to the project baffled Abdoulaye and may have provided that extra firepower that kept him moving forward. The corporation later sent in an educational specialist from Montreal, Canada, to evaluate the project. He wrote a favourable report of the school.

"It was uncanny. All the officials who'd visited the school were hooked and fell in love with the school. They took to seeing that I succeeded, as if they were partners in the project. The lady who'd led the operations at the World Bank, Mrs. Mehita Sylla, was particularly committed to the success of the project."

The project was fast gaining in notoriety in Guinea and in the developmental circles in the region. Upon learning about the institution, the IFC head for West Africa, based in Abidjan at the time, took a flight to Conakry to visit the school. This cemented Abdoulaye's confidence and, consequently, his relationship with the World Bank. The visitor was quite impressed with what he saw, and Abdoulaye recalls his words:

"You will never have to lease or rent new property for the school. You will buy the locations and the properties altogether now."

Business relationships also improved. The commercial bank softened its stance and was more receptive to the project. "We shall fund all future projects," the local bank manager announced during a meeting in Abdoulaye's office. "Whenever you require funding, just come to us directly and we shall lend you the money. We no longer need to bother the World Bank, we will finance you ourselves," he said, with a warm and whimsical wink.

The Hamdallaye School Today

Hamdallaye School now has more than 2,000 students within its classrooms: 200 kids attend the kindergarten, 1,000 pupils attend the primary school, and more than 800 students take their classes in the seven secondary and high school years (sixth grade to twelfth grade). Thousands of kids have thus far passed through the schools: 733 children have been through the kindergarten, 4,547 have been through the primary school, and 2,808 have been through the secondary school. Impressively, 2,140 students have taken their A-levels at the school.

When I asked him why he had named the school Hamdallaye, Abdoulaye was thrown by the question. He explained that when he started out, he'd asked the gentleman he'd appointed as director to propose possible names for the school. He'd proceeded to conjure up a few ideas, all of which sounded like offshoots of many of the Catholic schools already in West Africa. The justification was that such names would guarantee enrolment because of the good image of the Catholic schools. "Instead of following them, why can't we just create our own brand name?" Abdoulaye had countered. "We need to create a new and unique brand name," Abdoulaye declared, despite sustained opposition from most of the board members.

"I said to the board members, 'Listen, the neighbourhood where we are located is called Hamdallaye. If we translate that from Arabic, it means Praise to God.' And that was that. We had a new name and brand. Later on, as we introduced the secondary school and the kindergarten, we changed the name to Hamdallaye Group of Schools."

Considering his success in building up a high-quality primary and secondary educational institution, most of us would naturally be curious to know if he will now set up a university. Abdoulaye concedes that many people have indeed prodded him to expand his institution and establish a university. The local commercial bank itself has offered to fund the expansion, should he consider it. Abdoulaye believes the timing is not right, though he is open to the idea should the opportunity crystallize. According to him, to build a great university, you need solid partnerships with other prominent international universities as well as an excellent curriculum. Despite the availability of funds, he does not consider building a university as a priority as much as solidifying his current success.

And he speaks from experience. Abdoulaye has, in fact, taken a stab at setting up a university. In 2006, he contacted the University of Sherbrooke in Canada for this purpose. An education expert flew to Guinea to meet with him after a few discussions, flanked by two of his close friends from Canada. The three gentlemen were incredibly enthusiastic about his project and were keen on helping him tailor the Sherbrooke curriculum to the location at Hamdallaye. But as fate would have it, the Canadian embassy in Guinea closed down a few weeks later, citing a number of issues with how the military regime managed the country.

Abdoulaye shares that he is still considering the idea. In the meantime, he has embarked on a variant of the university idea. He has now set his sights on professional and vocational education that students can undertake after their A-levels. For the past 4 years, the group has created a vocational training centre in the field of healthcare. The institution is already training nurses and midwives and will soon train laboratory technicians and medical officers. He has partnered with healthcare professionals, such as distinguished local doctors who have a strong reputation in the healthcare field. They currently manage all the technical aspects of the vocational training.

Takeaway:

- Despite remaining a major challenge in Africa, finding funds to develop a project is possible through government initiatives, NGOs, or major financial institutions. Interest rates (about 20 percent on average) unfortunately remain prohibitive compared to other parts of the world.

- Demand for quality education services is high in Africa with real prospects for businesses and non-governmental organizations. One in five children, adolescent and youth[1] is out of school and the situation is worse for girls.

- The online education platform represents a promising avenue for the future as an investment opportunity.

---

[1] UNESCO Institute for Statistics

Chapter II

The Learning Curve of Two Social Entrepreneurs

Ernest nervously took another glimpse at his watch. The month-old smartwatch he donned displayed 11:40. They had been waiting for over half an hour, and he was starting to feel uncomfortable. The air conditioner was set too low, and it was getting particularly cold in the room. To keep his mind busy, he opened the file in front of him. With his team, he had prepared for this meeting for weeks, and he knew the details of the proposal almost by heart. The secretary, a slim woman with an ageless face, stepped in to ask whether they wanted another cup of coffee. He asked for a second espresso. As she strolled away, Ernest followed her outside the room and informally enquired whether the minister was still going to make it to the meeting.

"Intshwarele,[1]" Ernest whispered as he tried to catch up to her in the corridor. He knew a bit of Setswana—the main local language in Botswana—and his use of local languages had helped him on countless occasions to break the ice during his career. "I was wondering whether

---

[1] "Excuse me"

everything was okay. Are we still having the meeting with the minister?"

"Ee![1] The meeting will indeed take place. We are just trying to find an elevated chair for the minister so you can start," the woman offered candidly in response.

"Ga ke tlhaloganye."[2]

"As the highest authority at the meeting, the minister needs to have a sitting position that is higher than the other people in the room. We are looking for a chair in the building that would accommodate the minister."

The answer took him aback. As he later came to understand, by protocol, the minister is supposed to have a high-back chair higher than everyone else's chair. There was no high-back chair in the room,

and a few people had been frantically searching for such a chair for the past 45 minutes so that the meeting could start.

---

[1] "Yes"

[2] "I don't understand"

The meeting finally began about an hour later, when they found a high-back chair. Ernest sat in his regular chair, dumbfounded by what he had just witnessed.

Ernest and John

Practical and straightforward is an apt description of Ernest Darkoh and John Sargent of BroadReach Healthcare, a leading African healthcare consulting firm based in Cape Town, South Africa. They say "no" when they mean no. They commit 201 percent when they say "yes."

What do these two individuals have in common? A white-hot passion for improving access to healthcare and social services for the most marginalized communities in Africa, commercially. The correct terminology is social entrepreneurship.

John says, "We are essentially social impact entrepreneurs, and this is the kind of contribution we would like to think we are bringing to a project. Our typical customers tend to be large-scale donors like the Gates Foundation, USAID, CDC, and other private companies. The only common thing about them is the fact that they are working to improve access to quality healthcare to underserved populations. In a nutshell, we work with development agencies."

Ernest and John are both medical doctors who graduated from Harvard Medical School and opted to set up their own consultancy firm instead of pursuing a career practicing medicine. I first met these two energetic individuals when I contracted their services for a project called Base of the Pyramid. Ernest and John have long been friends, right through medical school as well as Harvard. They constantly talked about what they would do differently to improve healthcare, and not just in sub-Saharan Africa, but in other developing areas as well.

When I asked them to take part in the interview that would eventually result in their contribution to the book, they instantly agreed. As soon as they begin to discuss or describe their work, your mind cannot help but make an involuntary shift, and your senses become incredibly heightened.

John was born in Taiwan from an American father and a Taiwanese mother. He moved to the US when he was 4 years old. Because of his father's job as a diplomat, the family also moved to lots of different places every 2 to 3 years. However, his first experience in Africa was as a college student working in Sierra Leone with the Red Cross. This was during the 1992 conflict and the concomitant refugee crisis. The civil war was raging in Liberia, and the far-reaching effects had spilled over into Sierra Leone, prompting a refugee crisis.

John says, "It was a life-changing experience for me because I was young and in a very remote location, in a village called Shibuema. I worked in a particularly rough setting; no running water, no electricity, taking bucket baths, and washing clothes in a river. It was a really shocking experience, and it formed the basis of my career decision, as a medical doctor and management consultant."

Ernest's parents are from Ghana and are both academics. They left Ghana soon after independence and settled in the US, where he was born. At age 4, the family moved to Tanzania and then to Kenya when he was 11 years old. He went back to the US for college soon after his 19th birthday and did his undergraduate studies there, after which he proceeded to medical school, and later earned a Master's in Public Health. He worked for a couple of years for McKinsey in their New York office before coming back to Africa.

Ernest's return to Africa was partly funded by the Gates Foundation where he came in as the operations manager of Botswana's National Antiretroviral program. It was a cutthroat kind of situation as he came from the private sector to the public sector. He had to adapt fast and figure out how to be effective in the new environment. His first work experience with Africa was informed by the fact that he was a foreigner in every country he has lived.

"I have been a professional nomad, and that of course has its advantages as well as its disadvantages. For instance, the fact that I really do not belong to any camp, tribe, or even country makes me trustworthy in the sense that I can be a neutral broker or be seen as a fair mediator. The disadvantage is that I have virtually zero political capital. On another front, I am also disadvantaged when it comes to some of the benefits of setting up new businesses or companies in Africa that are available to locals."

For instance, being a foreigner doing business, Ernest found that he is automatically excluded from many business opportunities such as government contracts. On the one hand, such directives are well meaning and completely acceptable. On the other hand, they can be self-defeating. Ernest believes these policies often exclude people who might bring superior technical skill sets, which renders the mission hamstrung so that it cannot live up to its potential impact.

To Understand the Business Dynamics, First Understand the Subtleties of the Culture

On one of their assignments, Ernest and his team had to spend several weeks within the premises of a government department. When he first trooped into the office dedicated to him, he instantly noticed the old metal garbage bin that had clearly seen its best days. From the look of it, that might have been sometime before the First World War. It was not the most picturesque of scenes. Well, garbage is not exactly the kind of thing anyone wants to be distracted by, but this bin was especially ugly with chewing gum stuck all over its rusty interior. He resolved at once to get rid of it. So, one afternoon he strolled across the street and bought himself a brand-new, gleaming plastic bin. He immediately discarded the old one. That ought to take care of the problem. Or so he thought.

For the next couple of weeks, he was in and out of the office. He noticed that his garbage bin was not being cleaned and had even begun to reek. *What is going on?* he thought. So he waited for the janitor to come along as he did his rounds.

"Hello. How are you? My garbage bin has not been emptied for a while. Perhaps you may have forgotten?" he asked in the most cordial of tones.

"No, sir, I am only allowed to empty government bins," he replied almost uneasy. "And that," he said, pointing to the plastic bin, "is not a government bin."

"What do you mean?" Ernest replied, trying to conceal his horror.

"A government garbage bin is defined as a metal bin with certain dimensions. That is not it, sir, and I am not emptying that," he said expressionlessly and in what seemed like a rehearsed tone.

Because the janitor had to follow protocol and there was no way Ernest was going to use that grotesque bin, they made a little arrangement. He would come every morning and empty the new plastic garbage bin into the government bin, and then empty the government bin into the big collecting bags.

"It was uncanny, but he did it anyway, even right in

front of me at times."

Ernest's third strange learning experience would come during the application of government tenders. Botswana is known for its extremely transparent tendering processes. The process, of course, had its criteria, such as the number of copies to submit, which font to use, and paper size, among others. If you missed any of the criteria, even font style, the application would head straight into the trashcan. Many of his colleagues and friends from other organizations would apply for government tenders, and as they filled out the forms they would make all kinds of suggestions and attempts to use better templates or improve the applications. Ernest would immediately raise his hand in warning; "Do not deviate!" he would say, knowing where such applications ended up.

A Workshop, a Meeting, or a
Get-to-Know-Each-Other Session; Your Call

Ernest's experiences were not so unusual, considering I had had similar experiences while in Gabon. One time I had a meeting scheduled with the general manager of a government institution. I was seeking regulatory approval for some of our pharmaceutical products, and every road sign pointed to this particular office. So I initiated a meeting as soon as I had a contact name.

I went in to meet with the contact, and because she had been in the position for less than a year, I sought to learn what kinds of plans or direction she had in mind for the institution. The purpose of the meeting, as I had pointed out from the beginning, was to get to know each other. We started chatting up, exchanged business cards, and settled in for the meeting after small talk. Naturally, I had the first question lined up, potent enough to stir up a fruitful discussion.

"Can I have a broad idea of the direction you intend to give this institution, since I understand that you have just arrived? Perhaps you can share some of your ideas," I said with a smile. She immediately raised her hand, indicating that she was putting a halt on that line of questioning.

"You indicated that this would be a getting-to-know-each-other meeting, so let's just stick to that, okay? If you have another question, you need to make another appointment," she said, as cool as cool can be, throwing in a glassy smile for good measure.

"And," she added, "when you make that other appointment with my secretary, make sure you call it a workshop and not a meeting because if you do, we will still have to set up another appointment," this time with a hint of warning in her voice.

I was confounded and immediately thrown off balance. The meeting proceeded after what seemed like an oddly long interlude, but I had to quickly adjust my line of questioning to ensure I stuck within the getting-to-know-each-other borders, whatever that meant. I could not muster a trace of any rationale behind this occurrence. Considering Ernest's encounter about the high-back chair for the boss, this seemed like the old chestnut; a king seated on the throne, and at a higher level than everybody else did.

It was as if a cultural nuance had trickled into the business setting. The scene with the metal bin signified a worker who was under strict microinstructions and was not allowed to think on his own when it came to solving a problem. He was clearly more beholden by the process than he was free to solve a problem. This was a subtle allegiance to the ironclad structures and processes by which many organizations are run all over the world. "The tail wagging the dog," as John puts it.

Institutional Characteristics

According to Ernest and John, there is certainly a cultural component to it, but the more exacting influence is institutional characteristics. They believe that there is an almost universal character that defines interactions with governments, even in more developed countries. It is normally characterized by a rigid, vague, and set way of doing things. In the private sector, some of those methodologies or requirements might not make sense, but on the government side, that is how everything is structured.

Many African governments acquired, or more accurately, inherited the structures of their former colonial handlers. Ernest notes, and quite rightly, that there are similarities between ex-British colonies and the Francophone countries as well. You are likely to see the same structures, names of departments, and titles in countries such as Kenya, Botswana, and South Africa. "African judges in these three countries still wear the white British wig," Ernest quips.

He notes that such structures are not designed for speed, innovation, and nimbleness. Governments plan to match the needs of an entire nation or population. In order to do that, they inadvertently resort to systemization and rigidity so that they can run things on a large scale, and—this may seem shocking—to provide mechanisms for extreme accountability. In fact, Ernest and John believe that a large part of what we encounter in the form of frustrating inefficiencies and protracted delays is actually a spirited effort towards transparency and accountability.

Ernest explains. "It might easily take 9 months to

procure a laptop in a government agency. For someone like me who has come from the private sector, I can have the laptop today! But think about it. The first thing a government agency will do is to put out a tender notice in the newspapers and whatnot for a couple of weeks so that everyone and their cousins can get a chance to apply.

"One officer will be charged with going through the 2,000 applications and do the first round of shortlisting, never mind that the criteria used to analyze all those applications might easily be a checklist with about 100 items. As a result, 3 years later there would be a good shortlist to work with. Therefore, you can see that this is an attempt to be fair. If governments were to allow me to buy a laptop in one day, I am most likely to procure it from a friend's store. In many cases, they are right; people will go and buy it from their friends.

"As you can see, they are actually trying to do the right thing. The consequence is that it ends up being impractical. The items, many times, do not arrive in any meaningful timeframe to be of good use. So people are forced to develop workarounds in order to actually get things done because following the process properly does not work. Therefore, despite the existence of official procedures, the workarounds or bypasses always end up becoming the dominant procedures."

They concede that, when you set out to do business in Africa, you will have to pick out the codes. You have to discover both the official systems and the unofficial systems, after which you will need to press the right buttons so that they can send you through the faster route. If you don't, you will be sent through the proper route, which of course leads through a swamp. They believe that government structures are purposely built to *not* be nimble, efficient, or fast because those could easily create all sorts of leaks that form breeding grounds for corruption.

The Cultural Aspect

On the cultural side, John and Ernest point out that the way government employees interact with each other—their incentives, rewards, and many other dynamics—is incredibly different from the corporate sector. While at McKinsey, Ernest worked in a tiny cubicle, which was more of a hot desk, as he refers to it, than an actual office. He did not care about the size or location of his desk because he was happy with his job. He was paid well, treated well, and did interesting work. When he first started working with and within government, he was struck by how everyone was obsessed with the size of her office.

In fact, Ernest remembers that there were prescribed

sizes, right down to the exact dimensions, that were issued according to one's position or level. Because everyone was not attracting McKinsey rates of pay, Ernest imagined, perks such as the size of the office played a compensatory role in bridging the gaps in job satisfaction. With one's role or position came the exact square footage measurements for an office in the rulebook, to which everyone had to adhere. "At some point," Ernest recalls, "they had to take down entire walls and redesign some offices whenever a new person was hired or promoted so as to enforce compliance."

Based on their own experience, John and Ernest believe that they had to find a way to work with the energy, perceptions, and cultural influences that may be found in the government hallways. They could not just throw our arms in the air and demand that everyone change their standards and policies before they could work with them. Coming from a different cultural experience—which includes the culture of the corporate sector—one's first instinct would be to throw in the towel or set ultimatums, which of course will burn bridges. However, it is a matter of understanding the dynamics and then tapping into the energies already in place to get the desired results. This is actually a general rule of productivity, or of leadership as a whole. John and Ernest state it perfectly: "You have to figure out how to help other people meet their personal objectives, and then how to redirect those energies to help you meet your own objective."

Business in Africa

In Africa, and indeed many other parts of the world, governments have a bit of a chokehold on business, albeit in varying degrees. With the exception of communist states that lean towards state capitalism, many countries have an actual or, at the very least, some semblance of free market capitalism. However, many countries' governments in Africa still have an almost overweening impact on the markets. John and Ernest observe that it is especially harder to do business in Africa without working with or at least factoring in the influence of governments.

They reiterate that most of the influences, or what may appear to be stumbling blocks, from governments are actually well-intentioned, despite the outcomes. For instance, when they establish professional employee quotas or slap heavy taxes on the importation of equipment or technology, it's to create more opportunities for the local suppliers or workforce. Despite the gains that may derive from such strategies, John and Ernest believe that the time is ripe for a fundamental shift in the paradigms that inform those strategies.

"Such strategies have a profound effect in the individual countries in terms of overall progress and growth. This particularly affects businesses that operate in an environment where the government is the dominant player, major customer, employer, has a major chokehold in terms of regulation, or where it sets up the entire operating framework for business in a particular industry. It's a significant impediment."

Social Entrepreneurship in Africa

Social entrepreneurship and humanitarian aid models are not mutually exclusive. John and Ernest believe that they are in fact on a continuum. There is still a place for aid and donor funding in Africa. Despite the prevalence and proliferation of social entrepreneurship in Africa and the developing world in general, John and Ernest concede that it is indeed extremely difficult to develop business models that work. It is particularly more difficult in the realms of health and social services. Price points, for instance, are especially difficult to determine because they are different across continents and even countries. Sustainable business models that make economic sense are extremely difficult to create when you are on the business end of the table.

John says, "The concept of entrepreneurship and

shared values at a very theoretical level makes a lot of sense. There are big social problems in the world, and if you can figure out how to solve them, you can be paid a lot of money. The idea sounds sweet on paper, but then the challenge is figuring out how to get someone who makes $3 or $5 a week to pay for a service that costs $20 to deliver."

Therefore, they concur that donor funding, despite the prevailing issues, can help bridge the gap if used effectively, such as seed funding or venture capital towards social entrepreneurship projects. These projects can then take over as long-term solutions and as donor aid phases out. As social entrepreneurs themselves, John and Ernest explain that a great deal of their revenue (at the time of the interview) comes from the development partners and donor agencies that pay on behalf of the customers or governments.

The end game, however, which is more sustainable, is to see their revenue models become more commercial in nature. They acutely observe that "social entrepreneurship is at an early stage, and so far, there are virtually no projects in Africa that have managed to scale." This, of course, is far from a resigned statement. John and Ernest have relentlessly devoted the last 14 years of their lives trying to run and scale their own social entrepreneurship project.

Takeaway:

- Cultural awareness is an important factor to consider while doing business in Africa. Spending time understanding and integrating the cultural dimension rather than judging them from an outside standard proves worthwhile. Specialized centers offer classes on African culture to businesses.

- There is always a way to ethically make the most of awkward realities in Africa.

- Dealing with governments requires a paradigm shift for people used to the private sector. Adapting at times to slower processes, delays in response time, or even ambiguity are some of the adjustments one may have to face.

Chapter III

Transformational versus Transactional Leadership

Ruka has not read Robert Rotberg's 2012 book, *Transformative Political Leadership: Making a Difference in the Developing World*, but within 10 minutes of our discussion, I couldn't help but notice that her thoughts on business leadership specifically pointed to transformational leadership rather than transactional leadership. Rotberg did a fine job of demonstrating transformational leadership by picking out four iconic leaders, two of whom were Africans.

As a management consultant working in Africa, Ruka Sanusi has the rare privilege of meeting African visionaries who are staking it out in the turbulent African markets. Her work allows for a great deal of interaction with business leaders in Africa where she often gets to discuss, among other things, their experiences and entrepreneurial journeys. "These are not really your next-door entrepreneurs, but visionaries who look at the continent through a very different lens and, as a result, become trailblazers in their own right," she says.

According to her observations, many of these people operate in relative obscurity and are often uncelebrated, but they have all put a dent on the continent as far as business and development is concerned. "They all have unique capacities, competencies, and even personalities, but in my view, one thing sets them apart—their leadership approach," she says with conviction.

When she first met Patrick Awuah, a Ghanaian entrepreneur and a visionary, he did not strike her as just any other entrepreneur. Five minutes into a chat with him, she clearly saw his zeal. "He was passionate about the next crop of African leaders and, therefore, has set his sights on educating and developing future leaders in Africa," she recalls. As she would soon discover, he was not all talk; Patrick is a man of action.

Leaving no doubt as to his commitment and passion, Patrick left his high-flying career with Microsoft in the US and returned to Africa to set up a unique leadership institution. This, he believed, is what transformation in Africa needs. He would later, during a TEDGlobal in 2007, seek to answer the perennial question of "How do we educate leaders?" His resounding conclusion was: the liberal arts. "The question of transformation in Africa is a question of leadership," he declared during the presentation. He embarked on his mission and set up the Ashesi University, based in the Ghanaian capital of Accra.

There may be numerous opportunities in Africa, but

there are also unique challenges that often obscure or stand in the way of such opportunities. "A lack of visionaries and action-oriented leaders in Africa has been our Achilles' heel. The education gaps and structural rigidities that characterize many African educational sectors have certainly been key contributors," Ruka observes. She notes that many African universities still churn out young leaders with great potential, but they are not equipped to apply themselves to handle the African business and economic scenario.

In 2002, Patrick set out on an ambitious mission to address this glaring gap in Africa's pedagogy. While many educational interventions tend to focus on quantity and other structural factors, Patrick set out to properly prepare the next set of young African leaders. He practically threw away the mold and launched a unique leadership institution that would produce the kind of leaders that could address the African context. From an educational perspective, Ruka recalls that there was not much fanfare when the informal learning institute opened its doors to African students.

With such a noble and intriguing project, one would assume that donors, funding agencies, and other stakeholders would be falling over themselves trying to get involved. But the opposite happened. They all pulled out their binoculars and watched from a distance, if they watched at all. Patrick had to roll the wheel up the hill all by himself in the initial stages.

The institution operated from a number of rented facilities in and around Ghana. With just around 30 students, it struggled at its onset and was soon running on fumes. "In fact, the institution had to take fewer students, but Patrick was determined to establish a strong educational platform for African students," Ruka recalls. He had to rely on donations from his friends and family to keep the institution running.

Naturally, Patrick had set high standards so as to

attract funding for the project. He was determined to build nothing short of a top-notch and high-quality educational institution. He rapped on doors and courted funding agencies, but many of them were hardly excited about the project. "There were moments when he was presented with the tough choice of diluting his original idea so that he could get some funding," Ruka remembers. All he had to do was either scale down or significantly rework his original idea to receive funding, but he resisted any downgrade.

Money was not a strong enough incentive for him to give up on his vision, so he forged on, sticking to his original goals and ideals. Not long afterward, well-respected donors came calling. They bought into the vision and offered to fund the institution as it steadily grew in size, impact, and prominence. But it was not until MasterCard Foundation's USD$12.9 million cash injection that the institution really took off.

The foundation, owned and run by MasterCard, was founded on the belief that the key to prosperity is through education and skills training. Their beliefs aligned with the transformational vision of the Ashesi Institute. Their funding helped the institution to construct and move into its own facilities in Berekuso, a tiny village just outside Accra. Its new campus on a hilltop is now arguably one of the finest in Africa.

Transformational Leadership

"Transactional leaders run about 90% of African businesses," Ruka notes. "It is not necessarily a bad thing, and most businesses get by with this kind of leadership." In fact, Ruka believes that more than anywhere else in the world, African leaders face tremendous pressure to take the path of transactional leadership. The constraints are not only economic but also societal and cultural. After all, it is the path of least resistance and one in which many African-led corporations work their way through most of the rigors of the African business landscape.

"There is absolutely nothing wrong with being a transactional leader. However, it is important to realize that the African business context is more demanding and requires business leaders to be transformational leaders," she explains. Prestigious international institutions such as the MacArthur Fellowship and the Elon University have since feted Patrick for his revolutionary work. The Ghanaian government also conferred on him the Order of The Volta merit, the highest recognition of service for the country.

A few years later, Ruka met a young woman who had just graduated from the institution, and it was such a moving moment for her to see the results of this great effort.

The Ashesi Institute is now well recognized and has since graduated more than 700 students so far. The fact that many of its graduates choose not to export their skills to other parts of the world is remarkable. More than 90 percent of its alumni work within Africa towards progress and transformation.

Takeaway:

- Africa has the second lowest spending on education in term of percentage of GDP[1]. The investment on education by local governments in Africa, however laudable, regrettably remain small in comparison to needs of the population.

- Paying for education remains a challenge for families in Africa, as they finance out of pocket 25% of the total national expenditure on education[2].

- Allow for some wiggle room in your strategy but never dilute your original goal and ideals for anything inferior.

---

[1] Derek Tsang, Politifact 2014

[2] UNESCO

- Do not fall into the fallacy that African countries (or other emerging countries) deserve inferior products and services because of their lower purchasing power. Be a standout.

Chapter IV

Dealing with Communication Codes in Africa

Aboubakar Coulibaly's early encounters with what he calls "coded signals" came while engaging with the authorities, and in what were more or less noncommercial settings. He takes a sip from his cold drink and laughs, mostly at himself, as he stops to recount one incident. At the time, he was kicking himself for not picking out the simplest of codes, and one that was practically staring him in the face. It was "the clearest and most apparent of signals" as his friend called it from the other end of the line when Aboubakar called him for advice.

His wife needed to travel to Senegal for a family function, but she had just given birth to a baby girl, barely 16 weeks old. The baby required extra travel documents, which they learnt meant a letter from the local immigration office. Therefore, Abou picked up his cellphone and called a friend who linked him up with another friend. Two phone calls later, he had a breakthrough and was directed to an office where he got all the help he required. He was instructed to collect the letter within 2 business days, which he later learnt was a record turnaround period for such applications. No matter.

"Hello. I am here to collect a letter—"

"Hello, sir," she interrupted him, beaming and too happy to see him. "I remember you, sir. Your letter is ready. Just a little problem."

"Oh, is that so?" Abou exhaled in resignation.

"The printer has no ink, so I am presently unable to print the letter," she said in what seemed like a rehearsed tone.

Unsure of what to do next, Abou stepped into the hallway and phoned his acquaintance, the one who had linked him up, for advice.

"You don't know? What planet do you live on?" he

admonished after a roar of laughter. "She wants you to *do* something."

As far as Abou was concerned, the officer had done no extra work or had to go out of her way to prepare the letter. All she had to do was deliver it. There was little to no possible justification for her attitude or position. But she had leverage. She stood between him and the letter.

At that point of our conversation, Abou stopped and smiled. "I can see the puzzled look on your face, and you may be wondering whether she asked for a bribe." He had clearly anticipated what was going through my mind, as all my antennas were blaring "red alert, bribes, corruption, tips," and any other synonyms that applied.

"Now this is very interesting. As you can see, my friend did not use the word *give*. He said, 'She wants you to *do* something.' My ignorance of the codes actually was a boon in a way. Because, 'do something' can mean anything. You read and interpret it the way you want, but you definitely need to do something in a context where a coded signal is thrown at you. Some people in this situation may consider giving a tip in the form of a small or large payment. As much as this is possibly the case for the vast majority of people, being an ignorant person taught me that money was not the only answer to this hurdle. The responses sit in a wide catalogue, ranging from a broad and honest smile, to initiating a discussion in her mother tongue or the realization through a further discussion that she has an elder brother who attended the same high school as you. Giving a bribe is to take a shortcut. Maybe this is why many people tend to prefer this route. I am not comfortable giving bribes. Hence I take a route that may be longer, but one that gives me peaceful sleep at night. Moreover, this is why it is important to understand that a code must not be systematically misconstrued as a request for a bribe. It might well be the case, but you'd be surprised how often you can get away without paying one."

Early Days

Aboubakar Coulibaly, or Abou as he is more fondly known, started out selling computers at Axis, a local Compaq Computer dealership, after which he left a year later to join Unilever Côte d'Ivoire as a brand manager. We later reconnected when he joined Coca-Cola where he worked as a marketing executive and got a chance to build his knowledge of the region with frequent visits to a few West African and central African countries, and also through living and working successively in Guinea/Conakry, Ghana, Gabon, and Cameroon. He was back at Unilever in 2004 as the country manager, based in Dakar Senegal. A little over a year later, he switched industries and crossed over to telecommunications. His first stop was Celtel (currently Airtel) in Congo Brazzaville where he served as the marketing director for 3 years before moving to Côte d'Ivoire to join MTN–the South Africa-based telecom behemoth–as the chief marketing officer.

Abou left MTN in 2010 to set up a consulting startup with an old friend. However, for the past 3 years, Abou has also been working as a regional marketing advisor for PSI (Population Services International). While he is based in Ivory Coast, his role also covers most of west and central Africa, which includes Mali, Guinea (Conakry), Liberia, Benin, Nigeria, Ghana, Senegal, Niger, Cameroon, and the DRC.

Abou now spends most of his time visiting the various countries and helping them work out ways to do more sustainable business. Most of the PSI offices are moving away from donor-based models to more sustainable models where the activities and services offered can continue even if they do not make any money. A great deal of his work now involves helping PSI set up the appropriate models and approaches that will see the organization achieve these ends in the various countries. That said, Abou was more eager to share his experiences of doing business in Africa with me right for the period after he set up his marketing management consulting outfit.

Setting Up Shop

Abou is incredibly positive about Africa's prospects in terms of doing business. He believes Africa is still largely virgin land or a land of opportunities. "Africa is still lagging behind other continents in terms of development, but it is quickly catching up. It is now a matter of when and not if."

In fact, Abou believes that doing business in Africa is a gamble, but in the sense that there are so many opportunities that the real danger is finding yourself on the wrong bus and ending up nowhere. The current challenge he believes is how to identify and arrive at the right opportunity amid the numerous opportunities that exist within the continent. It is like a tree full of juicy fruit, and the difficulty is figuring out which is the right one to pluck. Having the proper means as well as an understanding of the environment is vital in order to choose well and succeed.

"So, what you are saying is that it is a high-stakes

gambling game in which you have an equal chance of grand success as well as grand failure?" I ask in an attempt to distill his overall view.

"Exactly!" he exhales. "You have to pick out the codes," he warns. "You could be in the right opportunity area but never make anything out of it if you can't read the codes."

Abou quickly realized that he had to stay sharp and alert in order to pick out these codes, because if he could not, doing business in Africa would be incredibly difficult. This, of course, corroborates my own experience and the experience of many other African entrepreneurs that have learned the shortest distance between two points in Africa is not a straight line. The destination or target might be within arm's length, but in most cases, we cannot just walk straight towards it.

Abou had more or less a literal introduction to this tenet while working with a new client in the DRC. He needed a visa to go through different provinces within the same country. When you move to a different part of the country, you may be treated as if you just landed from another country all together. In fact, Abou was startled by the difference between what the country appeared to be on paper and what he actually experienced when he first began to work there. He advises that people should spend some time in the African countries in which they intend to do business before they set up shop. To illustrate how different doing business in Africa could be, he tells the story of how he happened once to spend more than 6 hours in a jail cell in relation to a simple ID check in DRC. To date, he still does not know why he was detained because he was never given any kind of explanation or reason when he was released.

As soon as we recovered from the bout of laughter after Abou's retelling of his 6 hours as a convict, I was reminded of a similar experience of an acquaintance who was not able to move between places within the same country or between two very close places bisected by a border. He had crossed the river from Congo Brazzaville to Kinshasa for meetings. He set out to return in the evening and then catch his flight back to Paris the next day. Plain, neat, and simple plan, right? He left his luggage and everything else he did not require for the meetings in the hotel in Brazzaville. As it turned out, a little political unrest ensued on that same day and he could not cross back to Kinshasa. He had to fly to Paris and then fly back to Brazzaville to collect his personal belongings. Crossing the river is a 20-minute journey, but he had to fly 72 hours to retrieve his luggage.

When Abou left MTN, he was persuaded that there

was a great need for sound business advice in the region. He had collected valuable experience and, therefore, teamed up with his friend to help businesses set up solid business plans, marketing strategies, and plans to achieve their long-term goals. He believed that this was the right move, because his experience and expertise matched the requirements of the markets at the time. Therefore, the prospects of success were quite high.

His first client was based in Congo Brazzaville, and he recalls that it was the kind of deal that one would expect for a startup. A friend-of-a-friend-who-was-a-friend-of-another-friend type of connection. The deal was a shot in the arm for the fledgling consultancy outfit, giving it a lifeline to establish itself as it sought to attract more clients. The deal had a significant impact on the turnover. However, Abou was disconcerted by the fact that close to 60 percent of the total inflows from that deal alone had to go to one of the individuals at the said corporation. That was, of course, if they wanted to secure their business for the foreseeable future.

Abou conceded that such deals were common in Africa, and tended to involve smaller companies. Management consultancy juggernauts such as Accenture,

KPMG or McKinsey can hardly make such deals because of their strict guidelines and structures that effectively close nearly all the possible loopholes. They would immediately abandon a deal of whatever size the moment they detect or even suspect breaches or potentially underhanded deals. For example, KPMG severed its links with SASFIN, a South African firm owned by friends of the then president. They had to terminate the deal, which would have seen auditing and consultancy services for the $1.1 billion-valued firm, because of the mere possibility of impropriety.

That is not to say that they are *not* caught up in similar scandals once in a while, but such deals tend to favor smaller companies that have one or two decision makers, who badly need the business, and can be arm-twisted accordingly. Abou's firm contained these three components in spades.

"That's where the codes come in. Even in Cote d'Ivoire, I knew many people who required our services. In fact, we would meet with them and discuss ideas and the possible ways in which we could engage or assist them. But then we were not getting any business. The coded signals flew right over our heads in the beginning."

This, Abou remembers, was the single most frustrating thing when they started out. Cote d'Ivoire is a small place, and you can easily know everyone within your industry or circles. Abou knew how to access the relevant people and had managed to pitch to nearly all the right people. Most important, he knew exactly how to help tackle all of their challenges and how to add value to their businesses. Sometimes, he would even run into old acquaintances and mates from business school who were running companies, and they would invite him to pitch or send in proposals. Still, he missed out on all the codes and, therefore, could barely secure any deals.

Because many of those people knew him personally or through some kind of networking, they couldn't just tell him the codes. And once he had figured out the codes, he would still have to deal with a fresh challenge: This game expected of him to actually take a front seat position, and any such "coded" conversations would have to be initiated by him and not the other way around. Taking an active or passive role in "coded" conversations were equally daunting tasks for him. Abou also recalls that eventually it became easier to get business from people he did not know than from his acquaintances or networks.

Coded Business Deals Are Zero-Sum Games

"This is how we shall structure the deal," the company CEO suddenly announced to Abou and his partner midway through the presentation. "Sixty percent of the face value of the total deal must circle back to me if you are to secure this business. Does that work for you? Do we have a deal?" he said, more stating than asking. A quick estimate in Abou's head revealed that the deal would result in a 20 percent or less profit margin, hardly worth the trouble. But they were in too deep to turn back. The CEO, a European in his sixties, was an old acquaintance of Abou's partner and, for all he knew, the deal might already have been worked out prior to the official presentation. A wave of relief flushed through him. Negotiating such a deal would have been incredibly difficult for him and he would probably have tied himself in knots before coming anywhere near an agreement.

"I am not making any judgment here, and people are obviously free to carry themselves and their business the way they want. But this is a color-blind zero-sum game, and you cannot win both ways," Abou says. "Taking shortcuts comes at a price, and not taking shortcuts also comes at a price. Whether you are Black or White, it does not matter. I know that we lose a lot of business opportunities because some of the requirements are simply calls for bribes and corruption."

He notes that there are frustrations on both ends of the spectrum when it comes down to cutting such deals. Decoding the signals can be frustrating enough, but so is the danger of sending the wrong signals. The discussion can be rife with landmines, ready to go off when triggered by a wrong signal. Unless all of the parties are expressly clear on the terms of the deal, down to the intricacies of the handouts, you both have to be on the same frequency to send, receive, or decode those signals. Otherwise, the discussion can quickly head south if you send a signal that is misinterpreted and instantly rejected.

A Collection of All Codes

I asked Abou whether it is possible to make a small collection of codes that people can learn and identify when used during the kind of deals he has seen. He says that would be difficult to do because different codes are used in different business environments and countries. One would actually have to be physically present in that environment to learn the codes, or, at the very least, one would have to learn from someone who has operated in that particular environment.

According to his experience in various business environments, someone will almost always be expecting something whenever there are a lot of unnecessary and protracted delays, which are always backed by flimsy excuses. According to Abou, unusual delays are usually signs, or codes, that you are to do more than just wait.

"Sometimes you get a call or an email to inform you that you have successfully won an RFP (request for proposal). Everything is now set, and you have been awarded the business. But then it is taking too long to materialize. You get all kinds of explanations or excuses that are neither here nor there, especially if they come from the same person or office. The boss is not in, the papers have not been signed, and any such explanations mostly mean that you have to go out there and seal the deal."

Abou advises that the only way to understand or handle the codes is to get in touch with people who have been in the country and have experience-based understanding of the context and might perchance have even transacted with the same firms. You'll have to be quick because such people will not only help you flag the codes, but also offer valuable advice on how to handle the deal in its entirety. He offers a philosophical view: "This is much like when you visit a foreign country and you'd like to go out for dinner, or take a short tour at night. You cannot rely on what you read on Google about the country or the city. You have to speak to someone who has a more holistic perspective that blends objective and subjective elements of appreciation together to give you the actual picture and advise you accordingly."

From a business standpoint, Abou thinks that there is really no organization that can provide this kind of information. There are no websites or books within which this information may be found. One has to reach out and network.

"Perhaps they shall read about these codes in this book," he quips with laughter.

Takeaway:

- Paying a bribe remains pervasive in Africa and it can sometimes be a requirement to access basic services from public institutions. Transparency International estimates that 75 million people in Africa paid a bribe in 2014[1].
- Don't be too quick to interpret a code as a signal of corruption. It may well not be.
- When the code is a call for a bribe, remember there are ethically compliant ways to deal with the issue.
- Do not be afraid to walk away if the cost far exceeds any short-term advantage gained.

---

[1] People and Corruption: Africa Survey 2015 (Transparency International)

Chapter V

In Africa, Never Give Out Something for Free

Sunil Gupte is a straight shooter. When you pick up his (cold) call, part of that discussion will involve setting up a meeting at your office. He will then quickly be on an airplane to your location, wherever that may be. With an intricate knowledge of the African distribution landscape, Sunil is your man if you as much as consider any distribution forays of FMCG[1] and pharmaceutical products into the continent.

He insists that his DNA is now 100 percent African, even though his name is a dead giveaway of his roots. He is a cultural and professional transplant. He has spent nearly three odd decades in Africa, dabbling in sales management and setting up distribution channels. His understanding of the continent from a corporate angle is without question.

But even this, he concedes, is not an advantage. "Not nearly as much," he retorts. "It is, in fact, an absolute requirement for any commercial ventures in Africa." According to him, all bets are off. Despite the numerous

---

[1] Fast Moving Consumer Good

opportunities within the continent, there are virtually no guarantees. Nevertheless, he still made a daring move to set up a new (at least in Africa at the time) and unique distribution channel in northern and southern Nigeria.

A Career in Distribution in Africa

When Sunil first set foot in Africa, he was struck by the conviviality of the African people. During our first discussion, I tried to interject and inquire if there might be a tinge of exaggeration in his conclusion. Wagging his right forefinger, he cut me off.

"No, no, no, no, no. I know what I am talking about, Ben. I can tell you without fear of contradiction that this has been my experience across all the countries I have worked and visited. I think it is hardwired into the DNA. In fact, it is only a matter of time before someone unearths this great scientific discovery and scores a Nobel Peace Prize."

He recounts part of his experience as a business director holed up in an office in London where he would cold-call many of the major multinationals to persuade them to set up shop in Africa. Many of them never returned his calls, a not-so-subtle sign of their utter disinterest. "It was a tough job. I was ready to take a physical appointment at a moment's notice, and in any part of the world. However, some of them practically slammed the door on my face."

Sunil admits that his business experience is vastly biased towards distribution and that his experience is largely in the sub-Saharan region. He singles out Nigeria and Ghana as two of the countries in which he has spent a lot of his personal and professional time in the last 25 years. He had prior, and mostly theoretical, knowledge about the African business landscape, but he was struck by the distinct and varying trade constructs within the different countries, even among neighboring countries.

"The growing economies were characterized by huge and expanding populations. There were a few hiccups, as is expected with many emerging economies. But it seemed to me that they were a force to reckon with. I think Africa will be one of the most significant opportunities of the 21st century."

In 1990 Sunil came to Nigeria and worked with Churchgate group in distribution, yarn sales, and commodity trading in Nigeria, Benin, and Togo. In the late 90s, Sunil joined Fareast Mercantile Group of Companies to set up its Ghanaian operations. At the time, the distribution landscape in Nigeria quickly went through a series of fundamental changes. His greatest challenge became positioning the company to take advantage of these changes. He was then moved to the UK as business development director. Afterwards, he set up the group's shipping, logistics, and financing office in Dubai before moving to Nigeria in 2008.

FMCL had focused on distributing a range of FMCG products in the north as well as the south of Ghana and Nigeria. Distribution of these and other essential goods across Ghana and Nigeria was absolutely critical. Remember, Nigeria was and still is the most populous country in Africa, comprising nearly 16 percent of the total African population. Even today, standing at about 193 million, Nigeria's population is twice as much as the second most populous country in Africa. Many estimates suggest that it is getting closer to the 200 million mark. To put this into perspective,

one out of every seven Africans is a Nigerian.

In Nigeria and Ghana, Sunil noted there were three main distribution channels: (1) the wholesale channel, which is the commercial backbone of Africa as far as FMCG products are concerned; (2) the key accounts channel, which represents the modern trade that includes major malls and supermarkets; and (3) the traditional mom-and-pop stores, which are a lot closer to many people. "After much evolution, this is where the Nigerian market stands today from an FMCG distribution channel perspective," he observes.

Through the Lens of Time

In hindsight, Sunil fondly recalls that in the late 70s and throughout the 80s, Nigeria was a land of shortages. Businessmen would regale their counterparts with stories about receiving payments for goods before they even left the port. Customers would put money into your accounts before the ships docked. Any wind of information, even the faintest of rumors, would trigger a rush for goods, and people would make advance payments based on gossip alone.

Though these tales were a tad exaggerated, he notes, "There was obviously so much money floating around from the oil and other industries and virtually no goods to purchase. We were shipping a lot of products into the country, and, therefore, our accounts were always awash with advance cash payments for goods. At the time, whatever you brought into the country sold well."

However, it is a different story today. Back then, Lagos was the distribution center, and 80 percent of the goods in the country originated from there. Traders came from Kano, Onitsha, Port Harcourt . . . all over Nigeria to get stock for their retail and wholesale businesses. Moving forward to the mid-80s, more traders streamed into the market, and competition suddenly heightened. Sunil observes that the market transitioned from a production era to a sales era. "You had to establish and also properly run your own sales channels if you were to survive."

In Africa, adaptation is the name of the game. Sunil learnt that strategic inflexibilities quickly become hurdles, as had happened to many African corporations, especially foreign entities. Pivotal moments may be as simple as picking out a new consumer behavior, like buying behavior, and adapting a suitable model to ensure the company gains from the trends. It goes without saying that to achieve this, you will need to constantly have your ears to the ground. Sunil knew that distribution is ultimately about the interplay between products, channels, and geography. Therefore, he had to get these elements right if Fareast Mercantile Company was to stay afloat.

Sunil recalls that there were about 100,000 relevant FMCG stores across the country, and every trading company at the time had to figure out how to get into each of these stores. The wholesalers only stocked the products they wanted and were not particularly excited about carrying new goods. "Trying to move our products through the existing distribution challenges was a daunting task, especially because we also had to keep one eye on our bottom line." This was a complex set of challenges for nearly everyone in the market. However, Sunil was not about to capitulate.

In the late 2000s, FMCL veered off from the common path and made a resolute move to build its own unique distribution channel from the ground up. If it were going to succeed, then it would have to develop a completely new distribution system.

The first 100 depots were created across the country using an entrepreneurship model where FMCL signed up industrious Nigerians who were willing to work but did not have the required capital to set up shop. It facilitated all the initial processes that were required to get the depots off the ground. The entrepreneurs would then undertake the distribution by themselves and work to expand it. The initial uptake was phenomenal.

Sunil knew that in order to survive and grow the business, FMCL would have to switch from a shortage-based strategy to a make-available strategy. This was the best way to position itself to benefit from the changes in the distribution landscape. It was an unusual strategy for a trading company that had traditionally brought in the products that would sell on their own. FMCL would essentially be the first trading company to open up sales branches, something that was strange and unheard of in the business circles in the 90s. "We were a laughing stock and object of ridicule in the Asian business community. Everyone thought it was a dumb and desperate move."

Desperate, yes, but far from dumb. FMCL was unruffled by their peers' observations and derision. The truth of the matter was that many distributors were struggling to keep up the dizzying pace of change accompanied by the ever-growing levels of competition. Nigeria soon came up under the radar of several multinationals as a potent market. Companies such as P&G, already global leviathans in the global manufacturing and distribution of FMCG products, were some of the first multinationals to make forays into Nigeria. Competition heightened to almost unsustainable levels, and every company was desperately trying to get closer to the customer.

Sunil and his team deftly rolled out the new strategy, which showed a lot of promise in the initial stages. Many of the new entrepreneurs quickly expanded and started investing in warehouses to stock the products and vans to distribute the products from shop to shop. They would redistribute the products to retailers, and because Nigeria was a cash market, they could collect the payments upon delivery. As a corporation, FMCL, of course, did not want to carry this risk all by itself.

FMCL carried out training, knowledge transfer, capacity building, and even managed their sales force so that they could streamline their operations. They created partners who became key distributors and worked exclusively for FMCL. Along the way, the organization learnt an important lesson: when people invest their own resources and capital, they will come out working, nose to the grindstone, to ensure it turns out a profit. Sunil thinks he might have come up with his own African proverb: "In Africa, never give out something for free."

Under his leadership, FMCL created a better mousetrap. The project was a great success for the organization. It had also created about 120 entrepreneurs who were now living a relatively comfortable life. The benefits, of course, also trickled down as these entrepreneurs in turn created jobs for sales managers, sales reps, and other support staff. The strategy paid off in the end, both in its bottom line, and by contributing to the society by creating employment.

However, this was not the end for Sunil and his team. Before they could catch their breaths as an organization, Nigeria was already turning away from a sales era to a marketing era. Supply of goods had superseded demand, bringing with it a whole new bag of challenges.

Takeaway:

- Never give anything away for free. By requesting even a small token fee, you build partners that are more committed.

- In Africa, challenges, obstacles, and market barriers could be shorthand for massive opportunities.

- Technology is changing the service and distribution (wholesale, retail) sector landscape in Africa, with several initiatives to adapt international models (Amazon, Netflix, etc) to the local purchasing behaviors (Jumia, iROKOtv, mPesa, etc).

Chapter VI

When "Yes" Means "No"

"The people of Ibadan are very diplomatic and don't like to offend anybody," the trainer said, almost in passing. As Feyi Olubodun sat through all the data analysis sessions, furiously taking notes, his mind wandered for a few seconds. He was not sure if he had really heard that statement or if his subconscious mind was just having one of those noisy moments.

He had been involved in consumer research for some time now, but sought to polish his skills and gain fresh insights. After all, it was an evolving field and there was a lot to learn, even for the most seasoned professional.

The remark by the trainer was not really a profound or insightful observation, and certainly not a novel discovery. In fact, it was a well-known fact across Nigeria. "It is almost impossible to decipher if an Ibadan man is telling you no," he added. But even in his reverie, this well-known observation struck a chord with Feyi.

Ibadan is one of the most populous cities in Nigeria, second only to Lagos and Kano. About 3 million people live in the city, which is located in southwest Nigeria, about 120 kilometers to the northeast of Lagos. Feyi notes, "From a consumer perspective, Nigeria is divided into seven geo-political zones. Lagos is the central place that does not really belong to anybody. Then there is the southwest, the south, the southeast, north central, the northeast, and the northwest."

Understanding the African Consumer

For the last few years, Feyi Olobudun has travelled to different parts of the world, speaking about a model he has developed for understanding the African consumer. One of the videos at the top of search results for "the African consumer" on YouTube is one of his presentations on the subject to a Master's class at ESCP, a top European business school. All his talks are redolent of an intricate understanding of what makes the African consumer a little different from, say, their Western counterparts.

He has spoken about the African consumer across Europe, Africa, and the Middle East and is now working on a book that will synthesize his collective experience and the African consumer model that he has been developing over the years. Nevertheless, he still shies away from calling himself an authority on the African consumer, insisting that there is a lot to learn.

"What do you mean? You are an authority on the subject," I say to him.

"Well, you can say that, yes. I am a bit of an authority," he finally gives in.

Feyi grew up in southwest Nigeria, where he undertook his early education, and later went to Duke University Fuqua School of Business. His background was primarily in psychology, but he also undertook an MBA to expand his options. He is currently the CEO of Insight Publicis, one of the largest communication agencies in Nigeria. However, prior to his current career in communications, he was, for a number of years, involved in consumer research. He worked on several projects before finally switching to marketing communications.

His earlier work in consumer research at TNS RMS involved collecting and analyzing data from the continent and advising corporations that sought to venture into the African consumer markets. Even though he had worked on a few projects in Ghana, South Africa, and a few West African countries, he was primarily based in Nigeria. One of the multinational clients at the time had intended to launch three new drinks in the Nigerian market.

Therefore, when TNS RMS was contracted, product testing and consumer research was commissioned. Samples were administered across several locations to predict the potential uptake. The client's bottling plant was located in Lagos, which was the closest region in terms of road travel, just over 100 kilometers from the southwest region. The southwest region would therefore make a perfect ground zero for the client. A good uptake in the region would allow the launch of the products to benefit from lower distribution costs if it started out from the southwest. "I was instructed to pay attention to the data from the southwest," Feyi remembers.

The data collection concluded after a few weeks, and Feyi sat in his office for days trying to analyze and interpret the data so that he could make a conclusive report. "The client needed to know whether this product was going to be acceptable and where the greatest opportunity for product uptake was," he remembers. "So I was 100% focused on this particular task for a number of days."

But as the days ebbed away, Feyi was getting more and more confused. He had completed the analysis, but something was wrong with the data. He could not put a finger on it. By the third day, he was staring at the data, his face pale with concern. He phoned one of the data collection officers and requested to see a sample of the actual responses. Using the rear end of his pencil as a pointer, he carefully slid down each of the pages, scanning all of the responses, hoping to flush out any possible anomalies. There were none. The data was getting cloudier and more frustrating.

If he did not get the interpretation and analysis right, the final report would also be inaccurate. "I had never seen anything like this, and I was worried that if I got it all wrong, the bosses would flip!" Feyi had shared the preliminary results with some of his colleagues, and no one seemed to notice that there was something strange at play. They all agreed that a near-perfect rating for a product was not the norm, but then none of them could come up with an inkling of an explanation. Not even a wild or far-fetched theory.

At his wits' ends, and after a few more hours, Feyi picked up the questionnaires and started towards the records office. Barely 10 paces down the hallway, he threw a cursory glance at the questionnaire on the top of the bunch and something caught his attention. He slowed down before finally stopping in his tracks to reposition the whole bunch of papers so that it rested on the inside of his left forearm. He resumed his journey, 10 times slower.

With only two fingers, he slightly flipped the first sheet of paper so that he could have a peek at the second and then the third one, slowing down with every flip. Same thing—"Location: Ibadan." He stopped in his tracks, made an uncoordinated U-turn, and rushed back to his office, almost running into a colleague who was walking behind him.

He plonked the heap of questionnaires on his desk and furiously began to scan each of them. All the product tests from the southwest region were conducted in Ibadan. "We had tested the three formulations, and the respondents from Ibadan rated all of them equally, giving almost a perfect score," Feyi recalls. He could feel an answer to the quandary stirring up within him, an earth-shattering epiphany, but still nothing was forthcoming.

Then it hit him. His mind whizzed back in a flash to the training workshop he had attended 2 years before. The words of the trainer suddenly flashed in his memory. "The people of Ibadan are very diplomatic and don't like to offend anybody." A cultural nuance had woven its way into the data and would ominously have been used to produce an inaccurate report.

Saying "No" Can Only Bring Trouble

The people of Ibadan were well known across Nigeria for their diplomatic disposition and yes-yes demeanor. "They are a very diplomatic people. In fact, it is a common perception in Nigeria that it is difficult to tell when an Ibadan man is telling you no. They almost never say no directly. Instead, they will say it indirectly or tell you they will think about it or get back to you in a couple of days," Feyi recounts.

The trainer who had reminded them about that unique characteristic was in fact from Ibadan. "He had further indicated that the people of Ibadan thought it was rude to give anyone negative feedback if the person had showed kindness and generosity to them. If someone gave three products to sample, for free, people from Ibadan would not say anything negative in return."

They had perceived the product testing as an act of hospitality and not market research or product testing. That particular cultural aspect influenced their feedback and, ultimately, the data collected. Feyi recalls the sentiments of

one of the data collection officers: "When you give them the first product, they would say yes, it is good. When you hand them the second product, they will still say yes, it is good. They would then say the same thing about the third product as well."

A former African president used to say that "Saying 'No' can only bring trouble", as to illustrate that staying away from negative answers would prevent confrontation and bad blood. In other words, it was his own version of burying one's head in the sand. And basically, he would keep saying "yes," even when he meant "no" in order not to discontent other parties during political negotiations. This attitude put his political opponents through the wringer, as they could never correctly interpret whether he actually meant whatever he said or agreed to during conflict negotiations. He would make political concessions, fully knowing ahead that he did not intend to implement them. More broadly speaking, this attitude is a reality in some cultures in Africa. This is more a cultural orientation, more than out of ill intentions.

Feyi therefore had to discount the data from the region by giving it a lower weight. He would subsequently advise all future clients who intended to make inroads into the consumer markets of Ibadan to collect similar data from the surrounding towns and then analyze them together. Only then would they get data that makes sense and can be used for marketing decisions.

This experience taught him that even product testing can simply go wrong. Corporations can easily make the mistake of using similar results to launch their products. After all, inferences show that consumers are ecstatic about the new product. On the other hand, corporations can also conclude that such data is useless. But that is not the case. You simply have to take into account the socio-cultural influences and then compare them to other regions.

Feyi notes, "Nigeria looks like one big country, but it is not. There are over three hundred different dialects spoken in Nigeria and, therefore, English is preferred as the common multilingual dialect." Over the course of his work in consumer research, Feyi has helped clients to identify and work around regional influences that touch on culture and unique characteristics of the people.

These influences can be powerful and sometimes even transcend into firm beliefs that influence how that market perceives and interacts with your products. Feyi also experienced this firsthand. When he switched from consumer research to communications, he still flagged cultural and regional influences within consumer markets.

When one of Cadbury's distributors sought to relaunch their Bournvita brand into the Nigerian market, it signed up Insight Africa to help run its advertising and marketing campaigns. Bournvita, manufactured by Cadbury, the British confectionary behemoth, is a mix of malted drinks manufactured in the 1920s and sold initially in Europe and North America. It was later sold in India, Nigeria, Benin, Togo, Kenya, and South Africa.

The distributor had set specific sales targets for the different regions as one of the ROI markers for their marketing budget. "It was a major relaunch campaign. We were spending a considerable amount of money on sales campaigns, including advertising. We also collected and analyzed sales data from the different regions," he remembers.

Six months into the campaign, the sales data showed steady, significant growth in all the regions; except the southeastern part of Nigeria. Sales figures for that region were on a steady plunge, despite intensified marketing efforts. The first reaction was, of course, a rational one. A review of all the communication efforts was conducted with a view to establishing possible links to the outcomes. "We sat back and asked ourselves if we were using the correct media, whether we were getting enough coverage, and any other communications concerns," Feyi recounts.

No one could understand the trends. All the other regions were doing comparatively well, and the organization could not identify a reason for the steady slump in sales. Feyi knew that there was an underlying connection to the results, but he could not immediately draw any links. Therefore, he determined to unearth the source of what seemed to be an enigma. "Let me go down to the market with a couple of my team members and find out why people are not buying our products," he said to the client.

He immediately organized a few focus group discussions and customer visitation activities, and in just a few days, he had his answer. "It was ridiculous. When we went down to the ground, we made a shocking discovery. It turned out that in the southeast of Nigeria, there was a widespread apocryphal belief that if a pregnant woman drinks Bournvita, she would immediately contract malaria!" Malaria was, of course, a big problem in Africa, especially for expectant women and children, and therefore, it was a grave concern for the product.

By many estimates, the average birth rate for a Nigerian woman is about four to six times, and is particularly high in the southwest region. Before getting pregnant, a woman would consume Bournvita, but as soon as she had conceived, she would immediately stop. She would then switch to other competing products, such as Nestle Milo, taking her entire family with her.

The younger women believed much of what the

older women said. They took it as absolute truth and hardly questioned their opinions or authority. "Someone had in the past drank Bournvita and later on caught malaria. And since education was not strong at the time, she associated Bournvita with malaria. This then slowly spread out and was taken up as a strong belief, later to be passed down to the next generation," Feyi discovered. A 2013 National Demographic and Health Survey report that was conducted a few years earlier there indicated that nearly 40 percent of women aged 15 to 49 had no education.

"Nigeria is a very hierarchical society. People tend to ascribe a lot of authority and credibility to age, and, therefore, such beliefs can be powerful and widespread before anyone stands up to challenge them. It is likely that someone may have spread the word that, if you want to avoid malaria when you are pregnant, avoid Bournvita."

The belief was not only widespread but also firmly etched into the core of the people's minds. Feyi and his team then hit up on the idea to use an influential elderly woman as a direct ambush on this erroneous and widespread belief. "She was considered a social influencer, and she also happened to be a popular Nollywood actress," Feyi recalls. A running road show was set up, and she went across the southeast region trying to dispel the ridiculous myth. She would go from city to city saying, "This is not true, and drinking Bournvita does not cause malaria. Together with other pregnant women, she would proceed to drink Bournvita in public and say or take other actions in an effort to dispel the popular belief."

Takeaway:

- Cultural influences can skew rigorous market data analysis in Africa. Reading the data through a local lens is required.
- Seeking local expertise to better interpret market information is a must.

Chapter VII

Putting the Cart before the Horse

It finally dawned on Daniel that it was time to set plan B into motion. He had to act fast as the walls at Apex Developers Limited were steadily closing in on him. He had just moved his family back to Ghana, and he would need to find a way to keep the wolf out of the door. The inchoate real estate outfit had undergone a tumultuous 6 months, making a series of unfortunate turns. Daniel was the lone voice of reason within the corporation, secretly hoping it would change course before grinding to a fatal halt.

With a stellar education and an illustrious career in the US, it was not difficult for Daniel to secure a teaching engagement with one of the top universities in Accra. This kept his head above water as he laid the groundwork for what would later be a successful private architectural practice.

Apex Developers had only recently lured Daniel back to the West African city of Accra. Ekow, the sole proprietor of Apex Developers, had quickly pieced together a decent 2-year deal as soon as Daniel warmed up to the organization following months of back-and-forth communication. Up until that moment, Daniel was pretty

125

much standing on the edge of the cliff. He had been considering a move back to Ghana, and this opportunity was the final nudge that made him jump. After all, most of the board members, including the professor, were all professionals with impeccable reputations and credibility. It never occurred to Daniel that this would not be a solid move.

"Real estate is about capital and land. Without these two fundamental elements, no development projects or construction can take place. Apex Developers seemed to have these two elements in spades, at least according to the initial communications," Daniel explained.

Daniel had been mulling over a return to Ghana for quite some time. He did not have a clear or concrete plan, but his mind chewed on the idea, month after month. A Christmas holiday in 2007 became the pivotal moment that essentially reorganized his entire career.

In late 2007, the West African nation of Ghana was, one would say, awash with money from the mining boom. Oil had also just been discovered, and though it would not be ready for export for another 5 years, it stirred up the economy. Not least of the effects included a steady economic growth of 8 percent p.a., which sometimes spiked to 14 percent. Ekow was one of the investors who had earlier cashed in on the boom that had eventually paid off handsomely. With boatloads of cash in the bank, many investors sought to explore opportunities in other industries. Ekow founded Apex Developers and took aim at the fast-growing Ghanaian real estate sector.

Coming Back to Ghana

Daniel was not a stranger to Ghana. He was born and brought up in Accra where he undertook most of his early education. He went on to the University of Science and Technology in Kumasi to study architecture and soon after headed to Vancouver, Canada, to undertake construction management. He then took up several stints in the US, mainly in Washington, D.C., where he practiced much of his architectural career.

Even as a full-fledged architect with a stellar educational background and rather stable career path, Daniel decided to enroll into business school. His graduation from Kellogg School of Management ushered in a new era in his career. He took up more management roles rather than the usual technical positions. This new spin to his career would eventually bring him back to Africa. He left SE +Associates in Washington, D.C., to take a new role at PT Homes, a real estate company based in North Carolina, as a finance manager. One year later, he joined HH & R Properties in Las

Vegas as a property development manager.

In 2007, Daniel settled on Accra, the vibrant capital city spread out on the Atlantic coast, for his Christmas vacation. The trip doubled as an opportunity to look around for any opportunities ahead of his contemplated move. He was not entirely a stranger in Ghana as after all, he had lived virtually half of his life there, though it had been some time since he left.

The holiday was quite a revelation. He met with old friends for dinner and drinks, former schoolmates, and even colleagues and associates. Eight days into his holiday, Daniel ran into his former professor, an extremely polished and urbane gentleman. He had barely changed, a man-about-town who was highly regarded. Daniel was particularly fond of him back in the day, and when the professor proposed a casual meeting two days later, Daniel was more than happy to accept. The professor had obviously picked up some extremely important dollop of information from their small talk when they ran into each other.

"I am a board member of a real estate company based here in Accra. They are currently headhunting for a General Manager. I think you'd be a great fit, given your experience and strong background," the professor announced. Daniel's eyes lit up. A stroke of serendipity.

A recently established real estate corporation was

looking for an ideal fit to head their operations and help roll out their ambitious plans, and the professor happened to be on the board. Daniel was ideal in every possible way. Apex Developers was well funded and raring to go. It had a capital base of $10 million in cash, enough kindling to light a fire under its flagship projects. The local banks were courting the ambitious real estate corporation, ready to offer additional firepower if it met certain conditions. One of these conditions, Daniel learnt, was to bring on board the ideal management team.

Having worked for larger organizations with deeper pockets, this did not particularly stun him. Nevertheless, he was enchanted. At any rate, it was a perfect soft-landing for his return back to Africa. He was enthused that the professor thought he would be a great fit. Based on the professor's credibility and his position on the organization's board, all Daniel had to do was blink.

The professor arranged for a meet and greet with the company directors rather than a formal interview. Daniel finally met Ekow, the corporation's sole proprietor. He fondly recalls the vigorous handshake and the light squeeze behind the shoulder. With more years behind than ahead of him, Ekow was bustling with optimism. He was genuinely happy to meet Daniel and was practically welcoming him to the corporation.

As they made small talk, Ekow laid out his ambitious plans for the real estate sector, occasionally throwing in names of a few development projects that were about to take off. With a $10 million capital base and the capacity to handle projects that required several times the amount of capital it already had, Apex Developers was incredibly bullish about its prospects.

More meetings followed before he left for the US. Even after he left, the communication lines remained open and active. Nearly a year later, Daniel was finally persuaded. Apex offered him a decent 2-year contract where he would come in as the general manager. He packed his bags and, together with his family, moved to the coastal capital of Ghana.

All That Glitters Is Not Gold

As he settled into his new role, he was dismayed to learn the corporation did not actually own any land yet. There were a couple of ongoing complex land deals, but nothing had been secured. "I told myself there was nothing to worry about. Because the company had the funds to acquire the land, it was only a matter of time," he says.

But there were more unsettling discoveries, not least

of which was learning that his appointment was actually a necessary move for the corporation to secure additional funding from the local banks. The bankers had, in not so many words, advised the corporation to have the right management in place if they were to secure any additional funding.

As a professional, Daniel knew too well that availability of capital alone does not guarantee business success. According to him, this is "an elementary business tenet." Nonetheless, he settled into his new position, determined to look on the bright side and make a success of the venture. After all, he was now the general manager and he would be required to provide direction for the company's operations.

But this new piece of information lingered in his mind. It did not add up. "While the corporation had the wherewithal, in terms of capital, to see to its ambitious real estate plans, not a single parcel of the land was in the bag by the time I had officially reported for duty. And from a cursory assessment, none of the ongoing deals at the time seemed likely to materialize. This was not right."

The years 2007 to 2008 were a turning point for the West African country. Back in 1957, Ghana was the first sub-Saharan African nation to cut itself from the apron strings of its colonial masters. Now with double-digit economic growth rates and a burgeoning middle class, sectors such as real estate experienced phenomenal growth. Apex Developers was right in the middle of the real estate boom, and it was only a matter of time before some of its projects could take off.

Meanwhile, the corporation was quickly burning through its capital, and none of the projects took off. As the general manager, Daniel could not sit back and watch. Despite the glaring business mishaps, he had to work for the company. His first card out of the deck was to reach out to Ekow. He sought his full support to put on hold any activities for the project until the land was firmly secured.

"In effect, this was the right approach and pretty much industry practice. According to my professional experience, this was the most rational thing to do. Apex was losing a lot of its capital on operational expenses and overheads, which further complicated its risk profile."

Ekow called for an impromptu meeting to discuss Daniel's propositions. His colleagues were trained professionals and were not particularly enthused that Daniel was in the position to put on hold the only work on the drawing board (never mind that there was no guarantee for the land . . . that they were building a castle in the air). They blatantly opposed his propositions based on the industry practice which required the land to be secured before a full set of construction drawings were done for any project. There was a calm turbulence within the organization from the first day he reported for duty. The entire design team was jittery because they knew he could easily pick out any tricks. After all, they were in the same profession and would need Daniel's cooperation in any agreements they signed with Apex Developments, discounting the unprofessional approach and manner of service they were providing. However, their relationship with Daniel went from cordial to uncooperative when he refused a bribe.

Real Estate 101

Before real estate projects take off, the piece of land is first acquired. Then quantity surveyors, consultants, and architects all work to come up with the designs, initial plans, cost estimates, and a project business plan with associated financial analysis and returns. These services cost money, which had to be released in advance. Because 2 to 3 percent of a $30-million project was a lot of money, it was in their interest to develop architectural designs and drawings, even if there was no land secured for the project. The land acquisition deals took inordinately long periods of time, many of them eventually collapsing. They tried to get into prime locations without paying cash, and sometimes they tried to seal deals with institutional landowners such as the Catholic Church. Those kinds of deals are a lot more complex and usually take a long time to negotiate before any of the parties can commit.

Apex eventually folded. It became a matter of when and not if. Daniel had made his case against some of the operational moves, particularly the ones that siphoned cash out of the business. He opened up Ekow's eyes to some of the dubious dealings and questionable business decisions made by some of the people around him. Suddenly, it made no business sense for Ekow to continue with the business. He pulled the plug and ventured into other business concerns, and Daniel was out of work. Daniel of course had a plan B (teaching at a private university and setting up a real estate consulting firm) that he immediately set in motion.

In hindsight, Daniel recounts that he expected a lot of strategic management challenges when it came to doing business in Africa, at least on paper. He knew that the African business landscape has certain complexities that require unique strategic models. However, it was a completely different experience when he was right in the heart of some of the issues.

As far as he knows, Ekow had a chance to avert the situation and redirect the organization, to follow the right strategy. "He was a tad nescient when it came to the intricacies of running a business of such magnitude," he observes. Ekow had made his money through several mining concerns, most of which he eventually sold off to Newmont, the global mining colossus. He was looking to reinvest his money, and the budding Ghanaian real estate sector seemed like a great investment vehicle. Unfortunately, he had no experience in the real estate industry, much less in running a corporation of that size and scope.

Daniel insists that while morality was an issue it was not the only issue. The upstart and dishonest business professionals around him certainly contributed to the failure of the venture. However, he also believes that it was due to, at least in equal measure, a failure of following the right strategic model. Many investors discount the value of professional strategic advice and business expertise. The corporation had the capacity to run huge projects of between US$30 million and US$70 million. It could easily have been a home run.

The single biggest mistake was relying on the design team for strategic business advice. They were designers, engineers, surveyors, and architects—all technical people. They should not have been in charge of making strategic decisions. They developed designs and plans before the land was even acquired, essentially building castles in the sky.

According to them, the organization had a lot of money and they had to keep their jobs by staying relevant. To serve their interests, they pushed their designs and plans before the land was secured, putting the horse before the cart each time.

The African real estate market is challenged by a host of issues, ranging from corruption, dishonesty, and dubious consultants. It is not uncommon for service providers to lead investors down the hole so that they can serve their own interests. With a hunger for success, many professionals in the sector subvert the process to achieve personal gains. Investors are therefore forced to take extra caution before engaging service providers.

Takeaway:

- With the growing middle class in Africa, real estate developments grew exponentially in capital cities in Africa over the last decades.
- The offering availability of capital alone does not guarantee commercial success.

SUCCESS
USD
MONEY
BAG

Chapter VIII

If You Need Something Done, You Better Do It Yourself

The door swung open just as Narayan reached out for the handle. A middle-aged man rolled out, flashed half a smile, and scurried past him. The man was holding a small package, *Obviously packed medicine*, Narayan thought. Narayan was visiting the Sokoto branch of his employers, a leading MNC distribution house in northwestern Nigeria.

Narayan had worked earlier for a distributor who handled Beecham's range of products and had recently moved to the MNC distributor as a general manager.

"Nigeria was a maturing market with a vast pool of passionate and success-hungry talent," he recalls. "Anyone peering in from the outside might have been forgiven for assuming that some of the key managerial functions were known to all and sundry." It was of course a dangerous assumption, as he would quickly learn. "Most of the management functions were presumed to be known, but hardly anyone exercised or even executed them. Coming from a semi-mature market in India, this struck me as odd."

When he graduated from university in 1976, Narayan was burning with eagerness to apply himself. As a fresh-faced pharmacist, he landed a few stints with various pharmaceutical companies back in India. He had picked up useful and vital experience, a great deal of which shapes his overall work ethic and philosophy to this day.

It was then that he got wind of an exciting opportunity in Nigeria. In 1989, after nearly a decade of service in India, he spotted an opportunity in Nigeria, which was an unknown market to most people then. It was with an organization that handled the exclusive distribution of an MNC in Nigeria. With a lean staff of six colleagues, he took up the distribution that at the time spanned the entire country. They were turning out about 40 million Nigerian naira (equivalent to USD$7 million today) every year, a good turnover by 1989 standards.[1] A year later, the MNC scuttled the distributor arrangement, choosing to go its own way, which was when Narayan moved out to the leading player in pharmaceutical distribution in Nigeria.

A Journey To The Ancient Caliphate of Sakkwato

Narayan returned the smile and walked into the distribution center. Idogbe instantly recognized him and rose to receive him, waiting for him to come within a handshake

---

[1] 2016

radius.

"*Sannu*," Narayan offered.[1] It was perhaps the only Hausa word he knew.[2]

"Good morning, sir," Idogbe returned in crisp English. "How nice of you to visit. I was not aware that you would be coming," he confessed. "Shall we go to the office?" he said, turning to face the half-open door to the back office.

The Sokoto[3] branch also doubled up as a retail pharmacy. Idogbe had run the branch for 3 years. At 6' 2", Idogbe was imposing in stature and could come off as aggressive at a glance. But he was one of the most docile branch managers. He was a seasoned pharmacist and had done many job rotations at West African Drugs for close to 30 years. There were more years behind him than ahead of him, and he would soon retire. Narayan had met him a few times during the sales meetings.

Idogbe was a well-respected pharmacist in Sokoto. He had learnt the trade under the British system, a fact he would always reveal at the slightest of opportunities. However, when it came to handling the company's human resources, he left a lot to be desired. "It was not that he was inefficient, but he just could not seal up all the operational

---

[1] Hausa greeting meaning "Hello"
[2] Hausa is one of the tribes in Nigeria
[3] Sakkwato, modernized as Sokoto

gaps. I could not decide whether it was because of his age or that he could not be bothered. I settled on both these reasons," Narayan recalls.

During one of his routine checkups, Narayan had noticed an unusual order made from the Sokoto branch. "It was about 10 or 15 times bigger than the usual value of individual orders," he remembers. The order was executed through the sales supervisor and finally supplied to the customer. Idogbe's signature was conspicuously missing throughout the sales order. Narayan was wildly curious and made a copy of the order as well as a mental note to phone Idogbe at the earliest opportunity.

Narayan ran a monthly debtors' meeting at the head office in Lagos. As the reports were presented, the big, unusual order suddenly flashed in his memory. "There was a big order emanating from our Sokoto branch a few weeks ago," he cut in. He could not wait. "Has that been paid up yet?" he inquired.

"It has not been paid, but we are following up," one of the finance officers responded.

The debt stretched well into the second month, and there was virtually no information about the payment, much less about the customer. Narayan was alarmed. He immediately resolved to visit the branch. Two days later, he was on a flight from Lagos to Sokoto. It would be an interesting trip. "In those days, we had an airline that was just a tad more reliable than an okada, our local moto taxis in Nigeria. I chose the airline. With the right amount of luck, you would land in Sokoto. Otherwise, you would be forced to land in Kano instead and then take a road trip to Sokoto. If you ran out of luck, you'd probably circle back to Lagos if the plane had enough fuel."

This was not exactly the kind of round-trip one would envision for a short, local flight that should take roughly 3 hours. "In fact, the plane would more often than not turn into a multi-religious center where everyone would pray for a safe landing," Narayan remembers.

Safely in the office in Sokoto, he sat down his cup of coffee and reached into his leather folder, and then pulled out a copy of the order. "I'd like to know more about this particular order," he said, handing it to Idogbe.

A slightly puzzled look formed on the older man's face. "This one?" he asked, scanning the order. "Hakeem will be here shortly. He knows all about this order and why it has not been paid. He will give us more insight," he proposed.

"Very well," said Narayan.

Hakeem was the sales supervisor. He was responsible for pushing sales, making the deliveries, as well as collecting on those sales. He was key personnel for the branch and a perennial optimist, always vowing to close big deals for the branch. This particular order was certainly big.

After discussing a few other issues related to the branch's operations, Idogbe picked up the phone and called the said client. "To get more information about the order," he said.

Narayan balked. It had never occurred to Idogbe to call the client himself. He had relied on feedback from Hakeem all this time. He knew almost all the distributors in the area, but he did not reach out to the customer himself even after he had breached the 30-day credit period. He spoke in English throughout the conversation, and Narayan could pick out that the customer neither denied nor agreed that he had placed the order.

There was a knock on the door. It flung half-open before Idogbe could say, "Come in."

"Hakeem," he exhaled, stretching out his hand to indicate that he should have a seat. "Just the man we want to see."

Hakeem's face turned white. "Hello, sir," he said, forcing a smile as he sat down.

"Hello, Hakeem," Narayan said. Idogbe proceeded to ask questions about the order. Hakeem struggled to keep his composure. He tottered through all his responses, occasionally switching to Hausa, an attempt to elicit a sense of nationalism from Idogbe who maintained the discussion in English.

It emerged that the customer had indeed made an order, but that Hakeem had signed off on it and then had blown up the size of the order 10 times. He then diverted the extra consignment to his personal distribution channel, to be sold off later when the demand was high.

It was a tough lesson for Narayan, perhaps one he would never have experienced if he sat back and asked for a report. "A chance to make a quick buck often becomes a low-hanging fruit. Ethics are thrown out the window, and some employees will not hesitate to take a bite," Narayan observes. He further points out that "This is not an entirely moral issue, and I think as leaders, we ought to get off our high horses and address the underlying issues. We need to take care of the people and ensure they are getting the right remunerations, incentives, and bonuses."

Takeaway:

- This is not a story about business ethics, but about not taking a textbook approach when doing business in Africa. What might be taken for granted in another place is not necessarily so in Africa.

- Striking the right balance between delegation and appropriate checks and balances may be relevant in some instances.

Chapter IX

A Game Changer and a Well-Kept Innovation Secret

Patrick Mennesson was standing in the hall of La Grande Pharmacie des Forestiers in Libreville, Gabon, looking at the continuous flow of patients entering and exiting the pharmacy. He could hardly believe that with a small team of 15 pharmacy dispensers at the beginning of this journey 10 years ago, he had turned this business into the largest pharmacy in Africa, serving the need for medicines of more than 2,000 patients every day. No small feat, considering that Gabon is one of the smallest countries in Africa with less than 2 million people, far less than the population of many large cities alone in the continent such as Lagos, Cairo, Kinshasa, Nairobi, or Abidjan, just to name a few. For a moment, he smiled at the puzzled look on a patient at one of the counters who stood amazed at the speed with which his prescription had been served. The speed of distribution of the medicines, among other elements, was the well-kept secret behind the massive success this business had enjoyed for decades.

A call from one of the pharmacists, Dr. Eric Siehi, pulled him out of his waking dream. As he swerved among the customers in the hall of the pharmacy, Patrick decided to go and check again the secret he kept away from the patients' eyes on the first floor of the building.

A Jack Of All Trades

Gabon is a central African country with 550 miles (885 km) of coastline on the Gulf of Guinea, the part of the Atlantic Ocean creating a basin nesting all the countries from Senegal to Angola. It washes the coast of 13 African countries in the region and stretches over 6,000 km. The country is an OPEC member and a successful oil producer in the region, with an average output of 250,000 barrels per day, placing it ninth among the oil-producing countries in Africa in 2016.[1] Oil has long helped Gabon's economy, and its GDP per capita is the fourth highest in Africa at USD$7,530, right behind Seychelles, Equatorial Guinea, and Mauritius. [2] Gabon, along with Equatorial Guinea, are the only countries in the central African region with a National Health Service Fund (CNAMGS, or Caisse Nationale d'Assurance Maladie et de Garantie Sociale) to support its population's health costs.

---

[1] World Energy Council

[2] IMF April 2016 World Economic Forum

Patrick is a pharmacist by training, and he arrived in Gabon in 1994 as a trainee pharmacist. His initial plan was to stay for a couple months before heading back to his hometown of Montpellier. Little did he know that he would build his entire career in the country and become one of the forward thinkers in pharmaceutical distribution in Africa. His first assignment was in Franceville, the birthplace of the late Omar Bongo, one of the most revered and respected presidents in Africa. Patrick learnt the local culture in Franceville and also had his son in the small town.

"I have known Patrick for more than two decades now," recalls Gervin Landry Kah, Franceville's MP. "I remember a time when I was still a teenager and Franceville looked more like a small village than the city it is today with 110,000 souls. He used to relish visiting the villages in the district on his own and discovering the surrounding areas, and he also ran a small touring business for tourists visiting the region. I found him entrepreneurial at the time."

After an assignment as a pharmacist at La Pharmacy Moderne in Franceville, Patrick was offered a job at La Grande Pharmacie des Forestiers. The idea of improving the customer experience at the pharmacy had been on his mind since day one. It was clear that the demand for medicines in the country, as in most of sub-Sahara Africa, is enormous. A 2015 study by the management consulting firm McKinsey estimated that the pharmaceutical industry in Africa grew from USD$4.7 billion in 2003 to USD$20.8 billion in 2013, and is expected to reach between USD$40 to 60 billion by 2020.[1]

Building a Unique Customer Experience With Technology

Patrick explains his business. "Because we operate in a set and limited space at the pharmacy and because we face a continuously growing demand from patients, we needed to innovate in the way we delivered drugs to the patient. We found the solution in installing a Pharmax automaton. Pharmax is a small company based in Roquebrune-sur-Argens not far from Marseille and Nice in the south of France. It specializes in pharmacy automatons as well as other pharmacy-dedicated robots. The automaton is really a huge medicine dispenser with racks and an ejection mechanism that dispenses medicine packs to a conveyor belt, allowing for the dispatch of drugs to the specific counter requesting it at the pharmacy.

"The idea for using an automaton came to my mind

---

[1] Insights into Pharmaceuticals and Medical Products Africa: A Continent of Opportunity for Pharma and Patients (April 2015) -   by Tania Holt, Mehdi Lahrichi, Jean Mina and Jorge Santos da Silva

as early as 2009. I was on a holiday in France and decided to visit fellow university classmates to discuss my concerns. One of them pointed to an automaton as the answer to my questions. It was a solution that he had himself implemented at his pharmacy, and he was very happy with it. According to him, his automaton never broke down.

"The effective implementation date of the automaton at our pharmacy was February 2011. In 2015, we increased both the capacity of the automaton and the size of our premises. The automaton allowed us to serve a larger clientele, which required a larger space to accommodate the increased number of patients. So we can say that this is version 2.1 of our project since we increased both the capacity of the automaton and the size of the pharmacy to approximately 50 to 60 square meters.

"I have to admit that the initial phases of implementation were neither easy nor straightforward, and we had numerous reasons and temptations to give up. But we truly owe it to our colleagues who believed in the project and kept fixing the issues that arose during the initial setup and rollout. Now, the automaton we have in our pharmacy is the largest medicine dispenser our supplier has ever installed in the whole of Africa."

The automaton dispatches over 6,000 medicine packs through 12 dispensing nodes every day. In other words, about

10 packs of medicine are distributed every minute at the pharmacy, day in, day out. This is an amazing achievement, most probably a record by any standard and unheard of in the whole of Africa.

Between phone calls, Patrick tells me, "A lot of people regularly ask me how many jobs we eliminated through this technological innovation. And they are always baffled by my answer: The automaton actually allowed us to hire more people. We increased our staff from 50 before implementing the automaton to 160 today, as the increased demand generated the need to employ more people and provide a better service to our customers. The fundamental advantage the system offers is a significantly improved productivity for our staff and increased job satisfaction as they can really focus on strengthening the relationship with the customers they are serving."

Technology offers a unique opportunity to African businesses. Technology can make a quantum leap forward in growing businesses and offering better customer satisfaction. The example of Patrick Mennesson in Gabon is a case in point.

To the question that I pose next, Patrick takes a deep, hard look into the glass of water he is holding. "I am anticipating a time in the not-so-distant future when we could receive prescriptions electronically, handle QR Code prescriptions directly on our dispensers or provide drive-through services to our customers, considerably speeding the processing time for actually dispensing a drug and spending more time interacting with the customer for advice, answers, or hearing their feedback on how we could improve."

Takeaway:

- Technology is largely under-utilized to advance business productivity in Africa. Recent developments in computing offer vast growth opportunities to businesses and better access to markets beyond urban areas.

- Success stories such as M-Pesa to facilitate payments for non-bank account holders in Kenya, drone delivery of vaccines in remote areas in Rwanda, access to electricity through solar panels in Ghana are all vivid examples of the opportunities offered by the use of technology in Africa.

Chapter X

When the Road to Hell Is Paved with Good Intentions

Time was not on Mohamed's side. In less than 3 months, all the hides and skins in his warehouse in Khartoum and Port Sudan would deteriorate and become useless. A potential USD$2 million loss (approximately USD$3.6 million today) was giving him sleepless nights. Following a major announcement from the government to ban the export of raw hides and skins, it was clear that the prospects of Derma International were already circling the drain. And this loss would surely seal the fate of the once leading exporter of hides and skins in Sudan, unless he came up with a plan fast.

The Dire Economic Environment in Africa in the 1990s

In the 1990s, many countries in Africa faced a grave economic crises prompted by the fall in commodity prices, and high political instabilities with multiple forced regime changes and failed government economic policies. They turned to the bankers that governments borrow from for loans to support their fragile economies and budget deficits, as they have been for years now, namely the International Monetary Fund (IMF) and the World Bank. This time around, the loans came with a long list of strings attached in the form of structural adjustment programs (SAP) heavily championed by the IMF and the World Bank, pushing for the privatization of state-owned companies, deregulations, and reductions of trade barriers. As it was virtually impossible to implement SAP to the letter, governments in Africa put in place specific programs to try and keep the parts of their economies they perceived as strategic to the countries' economy away from the IMF and World Bank's fingers.

In 1993, Sudan was under great pressure from the IMF/World Bank. The financial institutions were threatening to suspend the country for not servicing its debt. The Sudanese finance minister was leading the country's efforts to win back the support of the international financial institutions and redynamize the economic prospects in the country. Several economic policy measures were launched in this spirit. And the ban on the export of raw hides and skins introduced in May of that year was part of the Ministry of Commerce's economic policy measures to boost one of its most promising sectors, the leather tanning industry.

On paper, the idea was simple and fit well with the aspirations of the government. The hides and skins industry was made of two major players. The exporters of raw hides and skins, such as Derma International, and the tanneries exporting processed or semi-processed leather. An end to the export of hides and skins was meant to protect the tanning industry, a concept in line with the government's objectives to move the economy from an agricultural and livestock base to an industry and manufacturing base. The move was intended to boost the local tannery and raw leather processing industry. A ban on raw hides and skins was considered the best tactic to drive the cost of goods down for the local tanning industry with the ensuing increased supply of raw material, thus making the processed leather exported from Sudan a lot more competitive in international markets. By the same token, the ban would raise the global revenues generated by the sector.

Less than 4 years old, the young government muscled its way into the industry, kicking and tossing, guns blazing, and essentially reorganizing the entire industry. "They had good intentions," Mohamed recalls. "But they took the wrong approach."

Derma International and the Hides and Skins Market in Sudan in the Nineties

When Derma International began its operations in

the early 80s, an FAO report estimated that there were more than 20 million cattle, 19 million sheep, 14 million goats, and 3 million camels in Sudan. Ethiopia was the only country in Africa that had a larger domestic animal population, with about 50 percent more livestock than Sudan. According to a United Nations report from the Food and Agriculture Organization (FAO), nearly a third of this livestock population in Sudan was wiped out by the August 1988 flash floods. Later, the 1990–91 drought and the effects of the long civil war further contributed to the reduction of livestock.

However, many reports today indicate that the livestock population has risen to around 140 million, and the leather industry today contributes close to USD$50 million to the Sudan economy. In the early 90s, the raw leather industry in Sudan was worth around USD$10 million (approximately USD$18 million today). The huge population of cattle, sheep, goats, camels, and other domestic animals drives the raw leather and hides industry. Sudan, at the time and before it was split in two, was the largest African country by area. Today, *Sudan* only refers to the northern part of the country, and roughly 37 million people live within its borders, sprawling across 1.86 million square kilometers.

Derma International, with more than half of the market share, was without question an important player in the industry. With a 60 percent market share, the company would become the epicenter of this shattering move.

Even with excellent storage conditions, and any amount of luck, you could only keep the hides and skins in a sellable condition for a few months. The government, through the shocking snap announcement, had effectively severed any export channels for raw leather.

Mohamed knew too well the official reasons for the ban. However, for a fleeting moment, he could not help but think that there were other motives than adding value to the industry as a whole. That there was more to the announcement than met the eye. He was maybe about to find out with the meeting he prepared to have with the Minister of Commerce.

Preparing for the Meeting with the Minister of Commerce

The move by the government was completely rational, and the idea behind it was well founded. However, the execution was a little too radical and not carefully considered. "Industry players were not even given time to pack up, clear their stocks, or honor existing delivery commitments," Mohamed recalls. With about US$2 million worth of stocks sitting at their warehouse, the government was essentially pushing Derma International off a cliff, and also looking over to see if it actually hit the ground.

The decision seemed to be cast in stone, and news about the law was all over the papers throughout the country. It was a questionable decision given that Sudan was, at the time, one of the major global exporters of raw leather. It was a steady and important partner to any organization involved in leather products and accessories. Ethiopia, Nigeria, Zambia, and Uganda are among the other African countries that banned the export of skins and hides. Sudan was one of the preferred suppliers of raw leather due to superior quality and the sheer volume it could churn out within a short period of time.

It was a long shot, but Mohamed angled himself to take it. He immediately initiated a meeting with the Minister of Commerce. Perhaps he could knock some sense into the minister and get him to rescind the decision. Or at the very least, he would try to persuade him to give Derma International and other industry players some reprieve during the implementation of the new directive.

Mohamed was a sober and astute business executive. When the responsibility to lead Derma International, one of the most influential corporations at the time, fell into his hands, he rose to the occasion. Derma International was a family-run and family-owned business, and Issam, one of his elder brothers, took over the operations in the Khartoum office. However, it was nothing like the usual mom-and-pop store by which we normally associate family businesses. As the name suggests, the corporation dabbled in leather products, both processed and semi-processed. It had dominated the industry for about one and a half decades. Derma International remained the top exporter of raw leather, skins, hides, and related products in Sudan.

Leather was, and still is, an important component of the fashion industry. The desire for leather in fashion goods spurred a global demand, and Sudan was on the list of top-quality suppliers. Therefore, the client list comprised fashion houses in Spain, Greece, Netherland, and the USA, among others. This impressive growth garnered a lot of attention, most of which was helpful. However, there was another group of people who were carefully watching this growth.

It is easy to assume that because it was a family business, someone would have to shake the family tree once in a while and one of the family members would then step up to lead the business. But Mohamed was perfectly suited for the role and needed no persuasion for the task. Derma International may as well have issued a formal job ad and gone through the traditional recruitment processes and they would still have ended up with Mohamed as the ideal candidate. He is an economics undergraduate from the University of Alexandria in Egypt and holds a double major MBA from the University of California. He also holds a diploma in Public Administration and Strategy Development from the University of Khartoum in Sudan, including a Six Sigma Green Belt Certification.

Meeting the Minister of Commerce

Mohamed arrived about 15 minutes early at Port Sudan palace for the meeting where the Minister of Commerce was staying in an official visit to Port Sudan. As soon as the minister learnt of his arrival, he called for him immediately. Mohamed was surprised. *A good sign*, he thought. Another aide emerged, offered a respectful greeting, and ushered him towards the gardens that had beautiful terraces overlooking the ships and the entire port.

The minister was a well-respected man with a PhD. He was sharply dressed, and Mohamed had to remember to use the Dr. prefix whenever he spoke his name throughout the proceedings. The fate of Derma International depended on this single meeting. Pivoting the business was an option, but one that Mohamed did not want to consider. As it stood, the new laws had virtually placed the corporation on life support. He might as well just have gone to the minister to request a more decent burial.

It was a delicate situation, and Mohamed could feel the adrenaline coursing through his veins as he walked towards the minister. It was a 20-meter walk that seemed like a 2-kilometer trek on a bridge without side rails. He finally arrived and stretched out his hand towards the minister, giving him a firm handshake.

"Salam Aleikum. Sabah al Khair," Mohamed offered enthusiastically.

"Aleikum Salam," the minister returned, flashing a half smile.

The rest of the men suddenly turned to look at him and cocked their eyes. He greeted each one of them, sprightly grabbing their hands and giving each of them a good shake. He could not make out if there was a previous meeting or if they had specifically assembled to discuss his agenda.

The minister called the meeting to order and turned to Mohamed. He laid out his right palm towards him, a sign that he should begin speaking immediately.

"*Shukran,*" Mohamed said, and went right into it. He laid out his concerns, the impact, and potential damage to Derma International as well as the industry in general. But before this, he lauded the new directive and pointed out that it was well in order and would certainly spur the local tanning and raw leather industry.

He finally requested a reprieve that would allow the industry players to at least clear existing stocks and honor all current commitments. "There are potential lawsuits from our customers if we do not at least deliver on the current commitments," he pleaded, trying for remorse. "My organization will do everything within its power to comply with the new directive, even under supervision," Mohamed vowed, watching for any signs of persuasion.

The minister stirred. He suddenly raised his arm, signaling that he had heard enough. "You need to understand that this will never happen," he declared, to Mohamed's surprise. The words cut through him like a knife through warm butter. It was not so much his refusal that piqued him, but rather the clear indication that there was no room for discussion or compromise. "There were undertones of annoyance," he recalls.

"This country is losing a lot of money because of people like you who are making a killing out of raw leather exports," the minister barked, looking around the table for approval. A few cohorts nodded in agreement. Instead, he believed that the country would benefit if the leather was tanned and processed or semi-processed within the country. He pointed towards the port and ships mid-conversation and declared that "not a single piece of raw leather will leave the country."

The tanning industry was, of course, a whole different industry, and Derma International was not in the tanning business. The local tanning industry was, by all metrics, still in its inchoate stages. In fact, Mohamed knew of only one tannery in the area, and its operations were somewhat spotty. Sudan did not yet have the experience and skills that could produce the right quality of processed or semi-processed leather. The additional transport costs alone, about 30 percent more, would significantly eat into the corporation's bottom line. The business would not be sustainable.

Mohamed never intended to get into an industry analysis with the minister, who clearly had a less-than-perfect understanding. One of Mohamed's chief aims was to get temporary reprieve to honor Derma International's existing commitments. Lawsuits and penalties would certainly come a few weeks after failing to supply what was previously promised. He invited the minister to visit the business premises so that he could see for himself the potential damage, but the minister curtly declined. As Mohamed would later learn, the minister had visited the premises that very morning. He had called on one of the major slaughterhouses in the city and had decided to extend his visit to Derma International. "I have noticed that your organization is still buying and stocking skins," he warned.

Mohamed was troubled by that particular remark. His family had built a successful business around hides and skins. It was not just their bread and butter, but also a key foreign exchange earner for the country. Because thousands of cows, sheep, and goats were being slaughtered every day, someone had to take away the skins. Derma International did this every day, and expected to keep on doing it.

"The hides and skins might still leave the country, sir," Mohamed responded, appealing to rationale. He was of course alluding to the fact that unscrupulous merchants will still want to satisfy the massive global demand for hides and skins. The porous borders would inevitably allow for smuggling of the raw materials.

He was stirred. "No raw leather, hides, or skins will leave the country," the minister repeated.

The meeting was over, barely 20 minutes later. "Shukran," Mohamed said. The minister's cohorts stood up one after the other, bidding him goodbye frantically. He started towards the door, hurried across the waiting room and towards the gates. The guards turned to him with a slight bow and opened the gates. He left the building, crestfallen and short of ideas to find a way around the quagmire.

The next day, Mohamed was sitting in his office in Khartoum. He had scheduled a meeting with Issam, his (now late) brother and his boss who worked with him at Derma International.

"He would have none of it. He is not going to give anyone a reprieve," Mohamed revealed.

"Walahi?" Issam inquired.

Mohamed recounted all the details of the meeting.

Issam turned blue. After a long pause, he spoke. "It is over, Mohamed, we might as well pack up, liquidate, and pursue other interests," he whispered. And he was right. Trying to pivot Derma International and invest into the tanning business would be an insurmountable task.

"As it turned out, the government had issued export concessions to a few companies that belonged to members of the ruling party. I had heard this, and even had hard evidence, though I never revealed this to the minister when I went to meet him," Mohamed recalls. "The beneficiaries had established these companies to export the same raw materials almost immediately after the ban was issued."

The fiasco was much bigger than Mohamed had imagined. It turned out later that the very tanneries that the government was keen to assist were sold to party members and other cronies. They virtually churned the entire leather industry, but for the worse.

Previously, the industry had made forays into key markets such as Spain, Greece, Holland, and the US, among other major buyers of raw leather. But only a few years later, these countries had looked elsewhere, and now the only key markets were China and India, much smaller markets compared to the previous numbers. The external market was not going to sit around and wait for Sudan to get its act together and resume exporting.

Of course, there have been global changes in the industry in terms of manufacturing and environmental concerns around the products. However, the grand plan was to pigeonhole the industry into a controlled channel that would ensure a one-way traffic for revenues into specific coffers. It failed miserably, and the government was left holding the baby. The FAO estimated the total loss from the ban at USD$16 million that year for all the countries that implemented a restriction on the export of hides and skins.

"Sudan could not regain its position in the global market even after the ban was lifted several years later," Mohamed remembers. It affected the economy in two main ways: a significant reduction in the total amount of badly needed foreign currency, and a near collapse of the supporting industries. After all, Derma International had exited the business and many of the other players in the industry had followed suit.

In hindsight, the ban was tantamount to giving away the shop to make a sixpence.

Takeaway:

- Arbitrary and not-so-well-thought-out government decisions can considerably add to the risk of doing business in Africa.
- Building strong political connections can help mitigate the risk of doing business in certain countries.

Chapter XI

The Color of Corruption in Africa

Adama was starting to lose patience with the Baye Fall who had been following him for the past 5 minutes asking for change.[1] The holy man had been bogging him down since he stepped out of his car parked in George Pompidou Avenue in Dakar Centre. Adama turned right when he reached the Sandaga roundabout. He went past the street vendors invading the pavement with their floor stalls on President Lamine Gueye Avenue. He stepped into the Roi du Bazin Getzner shop and started looking for a piece of cloth that would possibly make Madame Fatou Ndiaye happy. The owner, a middle-aged Lebanese woman sitting at her counter, kept reading her newspaper while one of the four male shop assistants attended to him.

"Hello," he said, strolling towards the item he liked. "How much for this one?" he inquired, not waiting for a response and pretending to look around.

---

[1] Baye Fall, dreadlock men with colorful patchwork garments and their calabashes are a common sight in Dakar, Senegal. Baye Fall are members of a brotherhood, the Islamic Sufi order. They do not own any wealth nor property and solicit passersby for their subsistence. They can easily be mistaken for mere beggars in the streets.

"Quatre vingt cinq mille francs, Monsieur. C'est une très belle pièce. C'est pour votre femme?[1]" the young man responded, scanning the unusual customer.

"Okay, I'll take it," said Adama matter-of-factly.

"Is there anything else you'd like?" the attendant offered, trying to upsell him and considering whether he should have asked for a higher price in the first place. Apart from bazin clothes, the shop was scattered with children's toys for sale. Adama wondered whether the seller had correctly guessed he had little ones.

"Non merci, ça sera tout," he replied, heading to the head-scarfed woman at the counter.

He paid and hurried off towards the door, the attendant calling out to him and flashing his receipt.

"Merci," he said, taking it out of his hand.

Adama tried to play out in his mind the possible outcome of the upcoming meeting with Mrs. Fatou Ndiaye, the head of the tax bureau in his company's district.[2] *How will she react this time?* he wondered. The meeting was scheduled to take place at 3 p.m., in about 3 hours. It would be an unusual meeting, but no less important. It would determine the fate of BigEye[3] Advertising.

---

[1] Eighty five thousand francs Sir. This is a beautiful piece. Is it for your wife?

[2] Not her real name

[3] Not the real name of the company

His mood soured once again. The holy man was waiting for him outside the bazin shop, grinning, and his calabash firmly in hand ready for some change.

BigEye Advertising and the VAT Problem

BigEye Advertising was a multinational advertising outfit. They had a small office in Dakar and had recently signed up Adama Ballo to head its Senegalese operations. The year was 2006, and he happily came on board as the general manager. "I inherited a hefty tax bill of about 600 million CFA (about USD$1 million today) from my predecessor." There was hardly any fanfare on his arrival at BigEye's offices. His in-tray was already full, and resolving the tax situation was top on that list. He might as well have been hauled in to specifically handle the tax issue, he realized.

According to the Senegalese tax laws, raising an invoice for services rendered automatically triggers the payment of the associated value added tax (VAT) to the collection authorities, which occurs on the 15th of the following month. Any advance payments received, which are common in the advertising industry, further compound the situation. They trigger the chargeable event for the full amount, whether or not an invoice is raised. "Because the regular payment terms with clients are generally over a month, a company becomes indebted to the Senegalese tax authorities before it can cash a single penny on any transaction it may have made, hence putting immense pressure on the company's cash flow," Adama explains.

BigEye Advertising found itself in the middle of a difficult situation, owing a huge amount of money to the tax authorities and not having the cash to pay either the tax due, or the associated penalties. Soon enough, the compounded penalties piled up, and everything spiraled out of control. "What a start to a new role as the general manager of a company! A million-dollar problem and virtually no way to solve it," he remembers. He was staring insolvency in the face, just days into his new job. "Negotiation was the only way out."

Adama set out on his own to meet with the head of the local tax authority and negotiate an arrangement to settle the matter. There was a designated Fiscal Service Center that covered the area. When he arrived at the Fiscal Center, he was directed towards a large lounge. The receptionist was incredibly upbeat, as if she had been expecting him, and had a permanent smile on her face. With the kind of issues that brought people to those offices, her presence in that office was something of a paradox, he thought.

"Monsieur Adama Ballo?" the receptionist called out. "You can go in now. Mrs. Ndiaye is ready to meet with you," she directed. The writing on the door said "Madame Fatou Ndiaye. Chef de Centre Fiscal." He walked in and immediately rushed across the room to shake her hand. She was a sprightly figure, and seemed to apply her makeup with a shovel. But to his surprise, she was amicable and listened attentively as Adama pleaded his case.

Adama recalls, "Over the following few days, we had several meetings, together with her two deputies, and we came to an agreement: BigEye Advertising would pay the tax bill in monthly installments totaling about USD$20,000 per year."

Adama was happy with this outcome, even though he understood that it might take forever to ultimately settle the total amount due. At least this would allow his corporation to stay in business and, at the same time, honor its existing and future tax obligations—a victory of sorts. Adama could now put this issue aside and set his mind on doing business and increasing revenues.

"I enthusiastically instructed our accountants to whip out the terms of the agreement so that the various parties could sign off on the agreed-upon terms. I even delivered the written proposal myself the next day," Adama recalls.

One week later, a bailiff officer turned up at Adama's offices to serve him with a notice. Something must have happened since he last visited Mrs. Ndiaye. The bailiff was in fact delivering a fresh notice, almost as if nothing had happened since Adama began the position. Adama was taken aback, considering how Mrs. Ndiaye had lauded him for coming forward and trying to find a solution. As he remembered it, she had said to him, "This is out of the ordinary. We are usually the ones paying a visit to taxpayers, not the other way around. Companies are for no reason overly afraid of the tax authorities and only visit us when they are forced to. Coming voluntarily to discuss an issue is not the standard practice, Mr. Ballo. Thank you for the initiative."

Adama immediately initiated a meeting with Mrs. Ndiaye, determined to establish what had caused the dramatic turn of events. As far as he was concerned, they had shaken hands to a deal that would fix the issue once and for all.

"You have to settle the whole amount, in full!" she announced as soon as he had settled in her office. It seemed he was dealing with a totally different person and spent the subsequent weeks trying to engage with Mrs. Ndiaye and understand why the agreement no longer held. After 3 weeks of shuttling back and forth, to and from her office, she would not budge. He was again at square one. "For a moment, I realized how stupid I was when I reached that agreement. It could never have been that simple," he recalls.

But there had to be another way. Mrs. Ndiaye was an amicable person and seemed reasonable, with her hearty laughter and almost endless bonhomie. *What had changed? What possibly could have happened to her?* he wondered. After emphatic pleas from Adama, she agreed to one more meeting. Adama's face lit up as he left her assistant and walked out of her office. An idea had sprung up in his head.

Many African civil servants barely eke out a living. Their pay packages and salaries do not reflect the general cost of living. For example, a high school teacher (Master's degree level) takes home an average of USD$227 gross salary in Senegal. A court magistrate earns USD$300 in Cote d'Ivoire. In comparison, a bag of rice, which would sustain a family for a month, costs USD$70 in both these countries. Rent and utility bills average USD$150, in a derelict neighborhood. Therefore, more often than not, they conjure up clever ways to close in the huge gaps between their earnings and the reality that is the cost of living. Unfortunately, some of those clever ways disrupt the normal course of business. Making ends meet in these conditions and raising kids is already a complex and difficult enterprise, let alone facing any kind of unexpected expenses such as disease or the arrival of a new visitor from the village. Therefore, the chance to make some extra money in the line of duty is an opportunity not to pass up lightly; an ecstatic summons to seal the financial holes.

Interestingly enough, the general understanding is that this is not really a problem since cost of living is low in Africa. I heard this argument over and over again from senior executives and Human Resource people, as a counterargument to cases I sometimes presented to request a raise of the low salaries of local teams in Africa. And the data they base their defense on is Mercer's Total Remuneration Surveys (TRS) on compensation and benefits around the globe. Mercer has sadly become the holy book in this matter. I am not sure how Mercer compiles its intelligence, but I believe their reports miss the point and eventually penalize African employees, as salaries in Africa documented in Mercer's reports are in my opinion not only not in line with the reality on the ground, but also serve as a tool to maintain salaries low. Mercer do not take into account cost of living impact on the measures they take of local salaries. Curiously, Mercer does also have a cost of living survey, which found in 2017[1] that *African, Asian, and European cities dominate the list of most expensive locations for working abroad.* However, Mercer's cost of living survey is designed for adjusting the packages of expatriates sent to Africa, but not to reconsider pay scales of the local worker. In a 2016 World Bank survey entitled "Is living in Africa expensive?", Shohei Nakamura &

------

[1] https://www.mercer.com/newsroom/cost-of-living-2017.html

Yuri M. Dikhanov concluded–in a similar fashion–that *despite their lower income levels, living in African cities is costly—compared with countries at comparable income levels, goods and services consumed by households in urban Africa are 20 to 30% more expensive*[1]. At the core of the debate lies, I believe, a simple matter of logic: Africa is a consumer market, not a factor one. People, like anywhere else in the world, consume rice, pizzas, bread, chicken, drink Coca-Cola and smoke Marlboros, drive in Toyotas, Peugeots and Skodas (even BMWs for some), and make their calls on iPhones and Samsungs. Almost none of these are manufactured locally as primary manufacturing, and are instead imported. So this begs the question: All things being equal, how much does someone pays for an imported car (and on which several taxes and duties are slapped) versus another buying the same car in a market where it is produced and sold locally? More? Less? The same? On the flip side, let's not also be naïve. We all understand the undisclosed ruthless reasoning behind the case for not increasing local salaries. It all boils down in the end to the P&L[2] as corporations are always looking for ways to increase

---

[1]
http://pubdocs.worldbank.org/en/571181466435029493/Nakamura-ABCDE-6-20-16.pdf

[2] Profit and Loss statement

the top line and reduce their operating costs, especially in African markets where revenues are often times smaller, compared to other regions in the west, or even Asian markets. It is fundamentally a catch-22 situation. Salaries are low because revenues generated in those markets are small, and revenues in those markets are small because employees (and therefore the bulk of the consumers for the companies doing business in these African markets) are underpaid. Companies are not charitable organizations and are essentially created to make a profit. We strongly support this tenet of capitalism. No doubt about it.

Perhaps a gift would help smooth things out during the next meeting, Adama thought. He was right as rain. Mrs. Ndiaye warmed up all over again, paving the way for a new deal that brought an end to the rift that had troubled BigEye Advertising for months on end. "My proposal for paying with installments was finally accepted. As long as we held out our end of the deal and made the monthly payments, the tax authorities never bothered us again," he recalls.

I asked Adama whether he thinks he gave a bribe. After a pensive silence, he replies. "It is open to interpretation, Ben. Look at the value of the pagne—about US$40—and the amounts that were due in taxes. Would that really count as a bribe?" he countered.

"But you had to give something for her to agree to

help," I said with a mocking accusatory tone.

"I really don't think so. The tax officials are also human. There was no way we would have cleared those payments in one big swoop," he said, determined to preserve his innocence.

Bis Repetita

Several years later, as fate (or luck) would have it, Adama was facing a similar issue with the tax authorities in his home country of Cote d'Ivoire. He had just set up his own advertising startup, and from his previous experience, he had taken pains to ensure that all his ducks were in a row regarding his taxes. Therefore, he had nothing to worry about when he got audited. But the tax authorities had other ideas.

"All our efforts to straighten out our books were apparently not enough. They put all our books under a microscope and, of course, found something they could use in the form of fabricated irregularities. We were slapped with a USD$100,000 fine, and suddenly we were under pressure from the authorities to pay up or have them pull the plug on our operations, not to mention some possible jail time," he recalls wistfully.

After weeks of difficult negotiations with the tax officer in charge of the audit, he was exhausted. This is when

Mr. Traoré[1]—the tax officer—felt he had put the right amount of pressure on Adama and went in for the kill, throwing a proposal on the table.

"The only arrangement I can think of will be for you to pay a third of the total amount in exchange for a 10% kickback," the officer declared. Adama was livid. He could hardly believe he was told straight to his face to pay a bribe to the tax officer. Without a steady cash flow, the only other option was bankruptcy. He was trapped between Scylla and Charybdis. He would have to relieve the 10 employees he had with him, many of whom supported their families through their jobs. Of course, the rapacious taxman, unruffled by his pleas for recourse, was not going to lose any

---

[1] Not his real name

sleep over his problems. "He had his eyes firmly fixed on the prize, and he was hell-bent on arm-twisting us into the deal," Adama remembers.

In comparison to the earlier ordeal in Senegal, Adama recalls that it was a lot more brutal in Cote d'Ivoire. This time, he was categorically and without any sort of confusion asked to pay a bribe. The tax officer unflinchingly demanded a graft, in cash. As he realized, in Cote d'Ivoire, the civil servant will usually display a more aggressive stance when demanding a payment of a bribe. He or she may in no uncertain terms make you understand that you need to pay if you are to make "progress" with the administration. "Give something" and "pay" are the common expressions indicative of the mandatory cash nature of the transaction.

"Who's to blame for this situation? I don't intend to cast aspersions, but the larger part of the blame falls squarely at our governments' feet. They have helped create the environments within which this malaise has sprung up and flourished. By not adequately compensating the civil servants, they allow for such practices to grow to epidemic proportions. In fact, some people believe that corruption is now a malignant issue in these parts of the world. It is hard to believe that civil servants can sustain families with the kind of incomes they receive. It is even harder to believe that the governments are unaware of the situation.

"It is my personal view that some governments have simply turned a blind eye to the problem, implicitly allowing civil servants to find solutions for themselves. At the moment, there is virtually no possible recourse when you are bullied or when you are forced to grease someone's palm in order to stay in business. While I am incredibly optimistic that the situation will improve, I also know that this is an ecosystem that has taken root. Therefore, I will not hold my breath for now, or at least for as long as my company exists."

As if being pressured from the top is not enough, businesses sometimes also have to deal with corruption on the other end of the spectrum—from their very own customers. Some of them also employ pay-to-play practices that ensure they get some money on the side over and above the transactional value of the deal. The moment you work your way to a long-term deal for some business or an order, some employees within the client's offices will want a piece of the pie. One of them once blatantly called Adama up in the middle of a public tender award process and happily informed him that he was quite ahead of the other proposals. They "preferred" his proposal, which perfectly fit their needs. And now that the business or the purchase order was nearly in the bag, they would require an upfront "gift" from him to seal it.

In this case, the systematic calculations of the amounts as well as the precision indicated that coercion had been the intention from the beginning. "It is a neat and well-planned script that is supposed to play out and produce a particular result, which of course, is not in our favor." With everything in place, Adama was, in fact, the unknown variable in the equation.

"So what happened? Did you end up giving a share of your profits to these unscrupulous employees? Did you report them to their management?" I was eager to know.

"Let's just say that, on one side, I found ways to get around the situation. On the other side, I have egg on my face. No judgments, thank you very much. And Ben, since I always enjoy sitting with you and having a chat, I will tell you everything regarding the way I dealt with this situation next time we meet over a cup of coffee in Abidjan," Adama replies with a wink.

Takeaway:

- Networking is paramount. Sometimes, it takes only a single person within your social or professional network to solve a complex issue.
- When facing an openly corrupt situation, consider escalating the situation in non-vertical ways.

Chapter XII

Keep Your Arms Where I Can See Them

The year was 2010, just 10 years since Nelson Mandela had been released from prison and 6 years since he had been elected as South Africa's first Black president. The Rainbow Nation was licking its deep wounds and working hard at turning the page on five decades of apartheid. South Africa held the African headquarters of many multinational companies, which considered the country as "not really Africa," as reflected by the modern infrastructures, the advanced social systems, and Westernized way of life. South Africa, five times as big as Japan, was home to the surgeon who performed the world's first human-to-human heart transplant in 1963, seven Nobel Prize winners, birthplace of Miriam Makeba and English author J.R.R. Tolkien, and was full of excitement with the preparation of its first Football World Cup taking place that year.

Dr. Allison Katlego had just taken over the reins of the South African operations of NewPharma at a time when business was flat and the company had hardly experienced any growth for close to 14 years. In fact, pundits and industry experts had all but concluded that the South African pharmaceutical market had already fully matured and perhaps complete market saturation was just around the corner.

Ally, as she is fondly known, had spent about 4 years at the organization in the Clinical Research Department prior to her ascension to the top seat. NewPharma was an A-list pharmaceutical company of repute, and if the new management she was leading could not do it, then perhaps it could not be done in South Africa. NewPharma would acknowledge failure in a country that was once depicted as most promising among the emerging markets, and would likely withdraw or scale down its operations in the country.

It would take less than 5 years to change that story. Ally steered the organization to new heights with phenomenal growth in both sales volume and profitability.

The organization, of course, got a lot of attention for its remarkable success, and continues to do so even today. The problem was that a significant part of the attention had to do with the fact that such success was seen as unlikely or completely impossible for an organization with an African leader at the helm. Success with such a leader, for some, cast suspicion.

"Since then, every single year, we have been investigated under suspicions that our business success must be due to some sort of extraordinary (illegal or immoral) explanation. I fully understand the need to maintain the highest standards in business ethics, and I know the issue will always remain a moot point for sure. Where is the line between keeping an organization in check and carrying on a witch-hunt? Hard to say."

Background

Dr. Ally Katlego was born and bred in South Africa. She undertook most of her education in top-notch universities in South Africa, which includes the University of KwaZulu-Natal for her Bachelors of Medicine and Surgery and the Wits Business School where she completed an MBA in General Management. She also briefly attended the University of Aberdeen in the UK where she achieved a Master's degree in Science in Clinical Pharmacology.

Ally is a medical doctor, and her professional career has almost entirely revolved around the healthcare sector, particularly the pharmaceutical industry. She is a renowned manager in the sector, and since 2010, Ally has been at the helm of the South African branch of NewPharma, a multinational pharmaceutical giant.

As I settle into my discussion with her, she is keen to point out what she refers to as a common myth that she believes haunts every successful African business leader. While it is not usually expressly stated, there is a quiet belief that no African business leader can enjoy enormous success without coloring outside the borders of business ethics. Ally, of course, finds this incredulous, but what gets to her is the sheer prevalence of this myth, both within Africa and without. Further, it is also often assumed that African business leaders mostly thrive in an environment of political uncertainties, which is linked to self-centered interests, and that their mind-set is not necessarily one that puts the interests of the business first.

Ad Hominem

The fact that the world stigmatizes Africa as corrupt when it comes to business is nothing new. A glance at the map of corruption in the world by Amnesty International shows nothing but red on the African continent. One-third of the bottom 100 countries for corruption in its 2016 classification are made of African countries, the highest proportion relative to countries from other continents in that segment.

Here comes the guilty by association fallacy: Africa contains some of the world's most corrupted countries. Therefore, any success coming from an African business must be done through corruption.

African business leaders working in multinationals have to constantly swim against this sometimes very strong current within their organizations, taking a considerable amount of time and energy. Knowing that they are being constantly watched, the exercise of putting extra attention to business ethics matters can become exhausting.

"In my experience, which I believe would be the experience of other African business leaders, catering to and responding to queries, and basically putting forth the extra effort to prove that you are doing clean business can easily eat up about 30-40% of your time. Your productivity will therefore be significantly hampered because you have to protect the organization as well as yourself from any potential implications."

Ally believes that with these kinds of issues making demands on a leader's time, organizations' African heads are strained to properly execute their duties, which include growing and steering the organization towards its goals. Meanwhile, their counterparts in Europe and the rest of the developed world are able to focus a great deal of their time into growing their corporations. To put this into context, Ally notes that it would normally take about 5 to 7 weeks to create a decent business plan. But with the constant badgering and demands to respond to ethics queries, it could take easily 12 weeks before one is able to do the same thing in Africa.

From her experience, African business leaders also have to put in several times more effort to be placed on the same level as leaders from other continents. They have to again and again prove themselves, even if they have been already successful in similar positions. This piles on to the amount of challenges that African business leaders have to overcome in order to achieve remarkable success. Fortunately, many African leaders have proven equal to the task. With steely determination, they have worked their way into business success and have placed themselves on an equal footing with their Western counterparts.

The general (and utterly wrong) idea here is that you cannot simply come into a market or industry and succeed. Your success will be all the more doubtful to other people who may have already been staking it out in the industry but have made no such success, or at least not to a similar degree. This errant perspective is fueled by the prevailing flawed paradigms that something has to be cooking in the kitchen for any African business leader to produce good results, especially if there have been none for an extended period of time.

In the particular case of NewPharma South Africa operations, Ally notes that, despite the relentless probes, to date, the organization is yet to be prosecuted or even served with as much as a formal subpoena. It has come out clean year after year and continues to prove that one can do business in Africa without walking outside the paths of morality and ethics or striking any underhanded deals.

As if that was not enough, this problem, according to Ally, is further compounded by the fact that some African business leaders still have to deal with disgruntled colleagues who also question the great outcomes that result from their efforts. She actually knows a number of business leaders who have had to undergo internal investigations in their own corporations due to so-called anonymous tips that amounted to nothing short of personal vendettas.

Where There Is Smoke . . .

In South Africa, for instance, Ally notes that the constant headlines that have to do with grand corruption and pursuit of political interests do not help the situation. These questions on ethics are normally justified by the emergence of such reports. Despite having a strong anti-corruption setup such as the National Anti-Corruption Task Team, South Africa suffers from a system that is patchy when it comes to enforcing its laws.

In a 2014 article, Gareth Newham, head of the Governance Crime and Justice Division at the Institute for Security Studies, pointed out that South Africa has dropped 34 places since 2001, according to Transparency International's 2013 Global Corruption Perception Index. He further writes that the Human Sciences Research Council's annual South African Social Attitudes Survey shows the proportion of people who think that tackling corruption should be a national priority almost doubled, from 14 to 26 percent in the 5-year period between 2006 and 2011.

The article by Newham on the worsening of the perception of corruption in Africa reminded me of the bomb

Ghanaian investigative journalist Anas Aremeyaw Anas dropped in 2015 when he released his undercover film *Ghana in the Eyes of God*. Anas filmed 34 judges and magistrates in Ghana taking bribes and incentives to twist the outcomes of judicial proceedings in favor of criminals. Anas who received several death threats, was to some extent luckier than Austin Okwor, an anti-corruption investigator in Nigeria who was shot multiple times in Port Harcourt, Nigeria. Okwor survived the attack, but reminds us that corruption is a matter of life and death for many in Africa.

Corruption is unfortunately not only smoke, but a grim reality. Branding the countries as corrupt, however, hardly helps because we often tend not to see the forest for the trees. I have always believed that putting in the same basket a government minister pocketing millions of US dollars for signing the grant of a GSM license to an operator and a nurse selling syringes to patients to complement her salary is somewhat unfair. Chastising a judge for making a thousand US dollars per month in bribes may be well placed when justice is at stake. However, the situation is not the same for the vast majority of small hands in the public services in African governmental institutions at the mercy of whoever can afford to give them extra cash to help them make ends meet and feed their families at home. I have met civil servants who are paid a hundred dollars a month and are then forced to carry on some level of activities on the side within the context of their jobs to raise their income. I have heard many people discussing corruption in Africa, but they've never had any contact with the people making a habit of accepting money in exchange for a service, nor have they tried to have a deeper understanding of the issue. The situation is not black and white, but instead takes into account a wide range of grey.

The lines become indeed all the more blurred considering that there is a case for cultural differences in the acceptance of "gifts" and other grafts meant as a sign of gratitude from the donor. I can think of countless occasions when people I interacted with felt utterly insulted because I had refused a gift they offered me. I know how sincere the gesture was, and it equally embarrassed me to hurt their feelings, but procedures and guidelines had to be followed. For now, the veil of corruption—both real and perceived—that covers Africa and Africans may take a long time to remove, at least for as long as most of the countries' leaders do not make drastic efforts to solve the issue in a holistic manner, and not only with publicity stunts.

How to Address These Issues

Ally sees two ways in which these issues may be

solved, or at least significantly palliated. The first, and perhaps the more urgent, one is to continue grooming more African business leaders. The idea is to completely fill up the talent pool with more well-trained leaders. This way, more African business leaders will come up the ranks and do business in the right way. Therefore, African business leaders have a responsibility and a crucial role in developing the next crop of business professionals. She notes that her current organization is fully committed and has in fact been able to demonstrate this commitment throughout the years. NewPharma has, on several occasions, received accolades in South Africa.

The second way would simply be to have an appreciation that no two countries are the same. Cut-and-paste strategies do not work in Africa—that has been clear to many multinationals who have made business forays in the continent. There is already a significant push, much of it from the West, to have a unified strategy or approach to doing business in Africa as a whole. Ally believes this to be especially challenging from an implementation perspective, owing to the different dynamics within the countries. Therefore, as a business leader, one should instead focus on having more African business executives who understand the environments in which they operate. In a way, this will be akin to lessening your business risk.

(Solutions) Made for Africa

Back in 2013, Ally attended a series of workshops where she represented her organization as part of the local pharmaceutical and trade council. She was not in the executive committee but still had to participate. A heated discussion ensued from one agenda, which touched on how to manage and deal with issues of intellectual property within the industry. A few brainstorming sessions later, the council arrived at some conclusions and a couple of propositions were agreed upon that struggled to go down Ally's throat.

"I have to say that the agreements and propositions were heavily influenced by, and were in fact generated by, a company in New York. This was not going to work for South Africa, and I made it perfectly clear. I mean, we had our political issues as a country but some of the propositions would actually come out as a coup d'état, and I was not going to be part of any of that."

Ally was the lone voice against the idea, but she stood her ground nonetheless. The council reached out to her later when the plan didn't work out, validating her point that copy-paste solutions do not work in Africa. She would later become a prominent member of the council.

Ally is concerned, to say the least, that even African

citizens themselves hardly believe that they can have their own credible business leaders. There is a widespread belief that African business leaders are in many ways incapable of steering corporations, whether local or foreign-owned, to the requisite heights of success that would command global respect. In my view, it may have something to do with the colonial mind-sets that the continent has hitherto tried to shake off. While this may be another argument altogether, I do believe it has an exacting effect on the overall paradigm of the African populace, particularly as far as commercial success is concerned.

Such paradigms become extra burdens to Africans with respect to generating their own wealth. Ally notes that, as a continent, we succumb too easily to the ideas and suggestions from the West in terms of what we should and should not do in Africa. This is also, as I see it, the case with many other developing countries outside Africa. It's a gloomy picture, but it's also a perennial reality that African business leaders have to constantly grapple with while doing business in the continent.

Doing business in Africa therefore becomes doubly challenging for the African business leader who will be under constant pressure to prove herself. She will also have to constantly fling her open palms in the air while working to show that she is not doing anything else under the table.

Takeaway:

- The general perception of corruption in Africa can put local business managers working for international organizations under a constant shroud of suspicion. Demonstrating transparency in all business dealings becomes for them a daily exercise and a factor of considerable stress in additional to business deliverables.

Chapter XIII

The Lawyer, the Banker, and the Entrepreneur

The crackling, digitized tune tore into the night and woke Elikem Nutifafa Kuenyehia up. A storm was thundering outside, and for the umpteenth time he promised himself to change this old-fashioned song that was his ringtone, despite how much he loved Kenny G's "The Moment"

"Who on earth is calling me?"

He had drifted off on the couch hours earlier for an afternoon nap, though it only felt like 15 minutes ago. He shifted heavily in an attempt to prop himself up. One could only hope for a wrong number at best or a relative who wanted to convey some sad news. As he ran over the options in his head, Elikem trudged towards the screaming phone across his bedroom. A recruiter? Perhaps one of his friends in another time zone who had the wildest of ideas to call and catch up? He found the phone, half-squinting as he picked it up to answer.

"You know what, Elikem? I have the perfect job for you," the voice on the other end of the line started with a tone of urgency.

"Hello to you, too, Funmi. I am very fine, thank you," Elikem wailed into the handheld, instantly recognizing the unmistakable contralto voice.

"I need you to take a pen and write down this email address," Funmi continued, ignoring her friend's attempt at being funny.

Elikem had written to his classmates, informing them of his decision to quit his job in the US and go back to Accra. Funmi had been one of the first school friends to reach out to him. She was from Nigeria, and now worked for one of the S&P firms in New York, and she had news. A prominent business mogul in Africa was set to expand his Nigerian banking business in Ghana, and he had just secured a banking license. He was looking for a startup team and would be hiring people in the coming weeks. Funmi had an enormous conviction that Elikem and this business magnate would hit it off.

"Nigeria, and banking, you said? Not interested. I beg you, don't disturb my sleep," he replied, suppressing a yawn. But Funmi would have none of it. She practically harassed Elikem in the subsequent days to at least give it a shot. They had been close friends back in business school, and she inveigled him, practically wearing him down with incessant phone calls, emails, and text messages. The running message was that he should at least meet with him. Elikem would eventually agree, more to shake her off than out of interest.

At the time, Nigerian banks in Ghana—and in Africa as a whole—had a bad reputation, so the idea initially struck him as incredulous. Up to that point, there had not been a single Nigerian bank that had come close to obtaining a license to operate in Ghana. Somehow, the businessman had managed to secure a license. Elikem was at least curious to learn how he had accomplished that.

ENK

Elikem, ENK as his friends call him, would soon turn 45. Among other things, he was incredibly worried about losing his hair and the fact that it was turning grey as the days poured into each other. "I am quite distraught about the whole thing, Ben," he blurts out in mock seriousness. "I am a single father to an adorable 5-year-old son called Prince Elikem," he adds, as if the two aspects were related.

Elikem was born and educated in Ghana. Both his parents were in the legal profession. His father started and ran a private law firm, dealing mainly in litigation, while his mother was an academic. She served as the dean of the faculty of law at the University of Ghana and the director of the Ghana Law School, the first woman to run a law school in Africa. She was later appointed to the ICC as a judge where she served for 12 years.

He undertook his early education in Ghana where he was cajoled into the science classes, or streams as they were called. At the time, if you were half-bright, you were encouraged, which was just short of forced, into taking the science classes and becoming a doctor or any of the related professions. In fact, his parents had a glorious plan for him to become a doctor. Halfway through his penultimate year of high school, Elikem fully realized that science was not for him. He jumped ship and took to the liberal arts, much to the horror of his parents and teachers. But he excelled and even won a full scholarship to pursue law at the University of Oxford. The scholarship took care of his tuition fees, living expenses, his flight from Ghana, and even some of the holidays in between.

He later went to the College of Law, London (now University of Law), and after doing his training contract at Travers Smith, joined Linklaters LLP's London office as a banking and finance lawyer. His plan, however, was to become an entrepreneur, but absolutely not the kind of briefcase businessmen he had seen.

"In Africa, we have what I call briefcase businessmen. These are men who run their business entities from their briefcase. If a car were to run them over on the streets and they died, that would be the end of their business. I definitely did not want to become a briefcase businessman, though all my training thus far was primarily in the area of law. I had to figure out how to start and run a scalable business without a shred of business training or knowledge."

He quit his job, borrowed $100,000, and set out to business school at the Kellogg School of Management in the USA, where we eventually met. Elikem focused on marketing, entrepreneurship, and finance. Immediately after graduation, he landed a full-time job at Diageo where he engaged in consumer strategy and brand management. But a critical aspect about the firm had escaped his notice before he joined. There was a quiet but widely held social drinking culture running in the company, never mind that he was a teetotaler. Unsurprisingly, this brought about a clash between his personal values and his job, leading to an enervating disconnect.

"I called it quits and informed my network that I was now looking for a job in Africa. Since I had been at Diageo for less than a year, I also had to pay back the signing bonus I had received."

At the time, Elikem was living in Stamford, Connecticut. But because he had lived in London before business school, a return to London seemed the most logical move. When he left Diageo, he shot out a mail to nearly all his classmates letting them know that he was currently unemployed and back in London and that he would soon be heading back to Ghana. He had all kinds of pressure to get himself back to steady earnings, but at the same time, his dreams and ambitions burned in him all the more.

He still had not fully repaid the money he had borrowed to go to business school and was tied up with the lease at his apartment in Connecticut. As he soon discovered, wiggling yourself out of a lease in the US was a near-impossible feat, even after one had moved out. Therefore, he had to pay his former landlord for the remaining months of the lease, unless he found someone to take up residency of the apartment.

For a stark moment, Elikem wondered if he had made a hasty move. It seemed unsound, especially as far as finances were concerned. The job itself was supposed to have been promising and an excellent start to his business career.

"The organization had recruited 10 of us from all the business schools in the US and was, in fact, grooming us to be its next generation of leaders. The idea behind the recruitment was that we were to work in various countries, including African countries, and then eventually work our way through to the highest management echelons. There was a lot of pomp and fanfare when we signed up. It was incredibly difficult for foreigners to obtain jobs in the US at the time, much less a six-figure salary with a promising growth path."

It was embarrassing for him to leave the organization. He had, only months before, informed the editors of *Kellogg Insight*, the business school magazine, about his new job and its marvelous prospects. Therefore, he hung his head as he informed them that he had since beat a hasty retreat and was now out of employ. But Elikem hung on to his decision, his values, and his goals.

The Meeting

During her many calls to try and persuade him, Funmi had pointed out how he liked to dress up and the amount of attention he had always paid to his appearance and grooming, and that the business magnate would most assuredly appreciate any such efforts.

"Elikem, I know you're always impeccably dressed, but when you meet him," she said, "go up a notch." The challenge might have piqued Elikem's interest because, two days later, he set out to acquire two new suits from Savile Row, a brand-new pair of shoes, a briefcase, a new pair of spectacles, and a haircut to boot. Never mind that he was still in debt, paying rent for his apartment in the US, and had no job.

"I had a wardrobe full of clothes, but I still went out to get new ones. It felt right. Talk about covering all angles in preparing for an interview! I looked and felt great."

The business magnate at the time lived in a penthouse flat in St. John's Wood, up in northwest London, and Elikem had agreed to an 11 a.m. appointment. A quarter of an hour earlier, he was standing downstairs, ringing the bell. No response. He pulled out his cellphone and shot him a quick text message. One hour later, still with no response, Elikem was pacing outside the flat, wondering if he'd got the address wrong. He tapped furiously on his cellphone as he sent messages to Funmi, nearly accusing her of sending him on a wild goose chase. He threatened to leave a few times, but Funmi insisted he should wait. "No, no, no, just wait for him," she begged. "Perhaps something came up. He will definitely show up."

Three hours later, a black sedan pulled up near the flat, and a sprightly figure of a man emerged from the backseat. Elikem stood transfixed as the man edged towards him. He stretched out his arm for a handshake as Elikem waited for him to say something like sorry I am late, or pleased to meet you, or anything to break the ice. Instead, Tony Elumelu looked him up and down a few times, from head to toe.

"Very nice, very nice," he growled, obviously impressed with his appearance. They went up into his flat and quickly launched into a bit of small talk as Elikem awaited eagerly for the interview to officially begin. He had made all kinds of preparations: background research about Tony and his companies, and a simulation of the kinds of questions he was likely to encounter. But there would be no interview, not in the usual sense of the word.

After about 15 minutes of conversation, Tony switched course. "Listen, it's really a blank piece of paper right now. Apart from the managing director, whom I have already recruited, tell me what role you would like. You can have any role you want in this new bank that we are setting up in Ghana," he pronounced.

At the time, Elikem was passionate about strategy and branding, which he had been doing at Diageo just before he left.

"Fine with me," Tony said with finality.

Before Elikem left his house, Tony had already spoken to the MD in Ghana, instructing him to prepare an offer for that role. Elikem was taken aback by his urgency and decisive nature. For a fleeting moment, he wondered if he had also done his background research and had already decided to sign him up ahead of the meeting, or perhaps they had just clicked.

Funmi had been right as rain again. Funmi is one of the main reasons I decided to join Kellogg, where I met Elikem. When I applied for an MBA, I was shortlisted for interviews in a handful of schools in the US. My initial inclination had been to go to Wharton where I had been accepted, because I already had some friends attending the institution. I hopped into a Greyhound bus from New York and headed to Evanston, Illinois, for my Kellogg interview. I was a little tired when I finally arrived but went on to visit the school in preparation for my interview.

After a brief, self-directed tour of the institution, I went in to The Atrium for a short coffee break. It served as the common area and school café. As I sat there reviewing my notes and basically trying to get myself into the right frame of mind for my interview, a youngish energetic lady suddenly planted herself on the opposite side of the table. She could have sat on any one of the many free tables surrounding me, but for some reason, she chose to sit directly in front of me instead, pissing me off immediately. I hardly took notice, or pretended not to, but I glanced up over my notes a moment before returning to studying them.

"Are you here for an interview?" she quizzed. Before a response could leave my lips, she made a lunge at me, snatching my notes without as much as an introduction.

"Yes," I returned, struggling to remain as polite as I could.

"Okay, let's begin," she announced as she adjusted herself on her seat.

"I'm sorry, what?" I gasped more in confusion than in shock.

She completely ignored my surprised face and proceeded. "Why do you want to come to Kellogg?" she demanded in a tone that suggested that there were 46 similar questions to come.

She searched my eyes for an answer, while I sat quiet and stunned for a moment before responding.

"Not good enough," she countered as soon as I had scrounged up a reply. "Try again," she instructed. The grilling went on for about half an hour, and she pelted me with all manner of questions I was likely to encounter during the interview, occasionally stopping to offer advice on how I should tackle each one of them.

"Now you are ready," she pronounced as she stood up to leave. She handed me back my papers, flashed a gleaming set of white teeth, and coolly walked away. My interview went well, and I eventually joined Kellogg, but that encounter in the cafe was precisely what I had been looking for. People who are supportive and do not even ask for your permission to help you. I ran into her a couple of weeks later, when she finally introduced herself.

Therefore, I was not surprised—not in the least bit—that Funmi would not only call up Elikem about the job, but also insist that he take it up.

The Job Offer

The new bank made Elikem an offer. He was to come in as the head of strategy and brand management. While he was considering it, Tony had arranged for a senior management retreat in Ogere, Nigeria. He had called the retreat for the team to chart the way forward in its African expansion. Tony wanted Elikem to get a sense of the corporate culture and the kind of people he would be working with so he was invited to attend even though he had not officially accepted the offer yet. It was a stimulating time for Elikem. Tony, in his foursquare and articulate manner, outlined his plan for dominance in Africa. Elikem recalls the manner in which all the senior managers were charged up and how they rallied around the strategy.

"We stayed up all night brainstorming and discussing ideas and strategies. No one even wanted to go out for a meal, lest they should miss a moment of the discussions. That went on for three days and nights in a row, and I had about two to three hours of sleep each night."

Elikem was so sold on the idea and mission that he wrote these notes in his journal. "I am drinking this Kool-Aid made by Tony Elumelu, and I am enjoying every drop. Good God, I would even work without pay for this."

When he first met Tony Elumelu, it was, to put it bluntly (and in his own words), "It was love at first sight." He was the most inspiring African business leader he had yet met at that point in time. His first instinct was, "I would love to work with this gentleman."

Reporting for Duty

Elikem turned up for work in Accra on the first day to what seemed like a project office, where everything was still dusty and helter-skelter. The managing director immediately sought to make him useful and tasked him with some administrative work. He sent him to sort out a car rental issue. He cheerfully informed him that an admin role had in fact been added to his branding and strategy portfolio.

"Admin?" Elikem gasped in horror. "I can't do admin," he announced regretfully. Given the way the term was understood in Ghana, Elikem was not sure he wanted it anywhere on his CV. Coming from a branding background, Elikem was hypersensitive about how roles and pretty much everything was named in the corporate world.

"Okay," the managing director growled. "Let's rename the role. We'll call it business services. Would that be okay?" he announced triumphantly and with renewed enthusiasm.

Elikem's role, therefore, expanded within minutes of his first day at work to become the head of branding, strategy, and business services. He did everything from buying the purchasing stationery, car leasing, and office rentals. Everything classed as admin. In a more exciting light, Elikem helped launch the bank to the general public in Ghana and handled all the marketing, promotion, and overall branding of the bank. As the head of strategy, he worked with a strategy consulting firm to write the bank's business plan.

The issue of compensation soon came up. From the look of things, Tony was determined to have him on board at almost any cost. Therefore, there was an immediate issue about paying him the kind of rates he commanded from his previous jobs in the US and UK markets. The bank couldn't pay him the local rates, but at the same time, as a Ghanaian, he could not be paid like an expatriate. It was his country of citizenship. Tony weighed in once again, and much to the utter chagrin of the MD, he negotiated a deal with him. A deal that messed up the numbers in terms of the budget.

"I was paid a higher compensation than I would otherwise have been paid had I been recruited locally."

The MD was clearly not excited with the arrangement. Upon a closer inspection at Elikem's CV, he realized that Elikem was also a qualified Ghanaian lawyer, so he bundled in a head of legal role into his portfolio. "I am not going to pay for legal services when we have a lawyer right here," he vowed as he threw extra duties into his portfolio. Elikem, of course, rebuffed the proposal, marking the beginning of the strained relationship with his boss.

"I didn't go to business school so that I can come back and be a lawyer, I thought to myself. He was only keen to get back at me, so I declined. There was already a budget for a head of legal, and this was just a ploy to ensure I was laden with duties that were commensurate with the kind of earnings I was getting. It was simply a way of getting me to do other people's jobs, but without also getting their pay."

Elikem on Doing Business in Africa

Elikem believes that Africa is full of opportunities, particularly for those who have obtained a top-notch education in the West. When he met Tony Elumelu, Tony virtually gave him a blank sheet of paper.

"You can have any role you want . . . take your pick," he had said to him.

At the time, Elikem had less than one year's experience in brand and strategy management, had never managed anyone, never worked in Ghana, and was practically a fresh-faced business school student. Yet, he had all these opportunities laid out in front of him as he went on to occupy some of the highest senior management positions in the bank.

This, he believes, also speaks of a type of African business leader, the likes of Tony Elumelu and his ilk. They believe in youth and in taking chances on people. It did not matter to Tony that Elikem was lacking the requisite traditional experience. In fact, Elikem later learnt that if his role had been put up in the advertisements or went through the usual recruitment procedures, the hiring managers would have required at least 10 years' experience. However, Elikem did not disappoint when the opportunity was conferred. This, he recalls, was one of the most exciting things he had ever done in his professional life.

"I lived on the edge of my seat every waking moment. I was so busy that sometimes the only time in my calendar that I could meet with anyone was 5:30 a.m. Some of the executives I worked with will easily confirm to you that I sometimes had meetings with them at 5:30 a.m."

Elikem fondly recalls one particular morning when one of his direct reports had promised to hand in a report before going home that evening. The understanding was that he would work on it before the end of the day and send it in. But then the executive had schemed to slink into the office early the next morning to work it up before start of business. To his utter surprise, he found Elikem in the office, in the wee hours of the morning. In fact, by the time he slipped into the office, Elikem had already punched in 2 hours of work.

Nevertheless, Elikem concedes that he was also driven because of the sort of person Tony was and his vision and ambition, which was incredibly infectious. It was certainly not about the pay, which at the time was only a third of what he had earned at Diageo. He enjoyed the exciting opportunity and the chance to participate in growing an influential organization from the ground up. The firm grew exponentially and won a few awards. This, he says, underscores the opportunities for talented business professionals and also the prospects for growth of African businesses within the continent.

The Beginning of Oxford & Beaumont

As the months flowed into each other, Elikem enjoyed his work, which was growing more exhilarating with each passing day. However, the company had imposed additional legal responsibilities on him. This meant that he had to interact with several legal firms in Ghana, which he did not really mind. But then he'd inadvertently got a sense of the kind of quality one could expect as far as legal services were concerned. One time, he recalls, a legal issue sprang up within the bank that the board needed to handle with a degree of urgency. His counsel was sought, and he had to engage one of the external lawyers. They agreed on the outcomes and the timelines. On the eve of the agreed-upon deadline, Elikem rang up the lawyer. He wanted to confirm that they were up to speed with the deliverables, and he needed to convey the lawyer's opinion to the board to make some crucial decisions.

Like many lawyers and law firms in Africa at the time, the external lawyer was a one-man band. He only had a secretary and a clerk. Unsurprisingly, nobody else knew anything about the opinion he was working on. Elikem could not get a hold of him and only later learnt, dismayed, that his cellphone was out of range. Three days later, he turned up, proudly announcing that he had attended an important function in the village.

"You see, I was installed as the new chief. I had to be there, sir," he reported in a repentant voice that also had an undercurrent of pride. "Network coverage is a big problem in my village," he droned on to a bewildered Elikem who was already 3 days late in submitting the opinion to the board.

When he finally delivered the opinion, it was shoddily drafted and did not answer the question it was meant to. Elikem immediately tossed it into the bin. He looked for the soft copy version and, using the Track Changes feature, made several edits and then sent it back to him for review and to find out what he thought about the suggestions. To his distinct and utter dismay, the lawyer accepted all the changes. Elikem jumped when the lawyer later sent in his fee for the work, lighting up a bright idea in his entrepreneurial mind.

Meanwhile, his relationship with the MD was becoming increasingly strained, and it was only a matter of time before it snapped. Elikem had grown up in a family of lawyers where constant healthy arguments were never far off and where everybody's opinion was respected, whether you were young or old. He notes that, in African cultures, there is still a lot of emphasis on hierarchy, which has seeped into the African corporate culture.

"There I was, 31 years old, a handsome and fresh-faced business executive, while my boss was a lot more seasoned with significant experience in retail banking. The expectation was clear; I was to tow the line, or more preferably, kowtow. My whole being revolted at the thought."

After a few altercations, Elikem finally opted out and resigned from his position. Tony detoured his private jet to Accra and tried to persuade him to stay. He grudgingly went back to work, but then quietly resigned again after a short period of time. He did not inform Tony this time around. Elikem had been at the bank for around 2 years, and suddenly he did not have the faintest idea of what he wanted to do with himself. Therefore, he chose to serve his 3-month notice as he tried to work out the next step. He still had the student loan to pay, and money soon became the urgent need.

One dreamy moment as he served his final few days, he hit up on an idea, which he admits was not quite novel but nonetheless represented an excellent opportunity. When the lawyer he had earlier contracted for the bank finally turned up after his inauguration as the village chief, he had delivered a less-than-perfect opinion. Elikem had then made all kinds of corrections and suggestions and had practically done more than half of the work for him. But the light bulb moment came when the lawyer slapped the organization with a $10,000 bill for his services.

"It immediately struck me that if a lawyer can get $10,000 so easily, then I was on the wrong side of the table. I was a qualified Ghanaian lawyer who had trained in the city of London. In fact, from a cursory assessment of the quality from lawyers and law firms I worked with while at the bank, I knew I could do a better job."

Elikem took his last paycheck from the bank and started up his law firm, Oxford & Beaumont Solicitors. Elikem picked the name as a homage to Oxford University, where he attended law school, and the street he lived on when he was a student, Beaumont Street in Oxford. He considered himself a "textbook entrepreneur, a low-risk investor who would not borrow much or go all out with other people's money." So, naturally, he was keen to start a business that did not require so much money.

"I started my own law firm with $5,000, the only direct financial investment I have ever made to date. The firm's growth has always been organic, right from the onset. Since I already knew the landlord of the building that the bank occupied, I negotiated for a small space on the 12th floor. My previous employer occupied the first three floors. I secured a 30 square meter (323 sq ft) space where I set up my firm, all geared up for business. I paid 6 months' rent and bought a laptop with the rest of the money."

The success of the bank opened the floodgates of the Ghanaian banking sector, and a flurry of other African banks sought to gain a piece of the action. Elikem recalls that, even though he had now left the bank, he was still at a very unique position. He had hoped to leverage this to consult for other investors who were applying for or had obtained licenses to operate in Ghana.

"One particular group of investors had just received an operating license to set up a bank to be run by a young and dynamic Ghanaian management team. One of my friend's cousins was part of that team, and I had gone through him to secure an opportunity to pitch my experience and services. I thought it was a shoo-in for me to support them in the strategy, branding, and legal matters."

At the meeting, the MD suddenly ambushed him with what felt like a series of grim questions.

"Aah, Elikem," he said, glaring at him condescendingly. "How old are you? How long have you been practicing at the bar? Why are you not joining your father's law firm?" he said in mock concern.

The words cut through Elikem like a cold knife, and when he left the building, he made a beeline to his small, new office. He had made little money in that month, so he pulled out his laptop and emailed a bunch of partners and friends that he had worked with in London. He had been lucky to have worked in a few exciting deals with them, including major restructuring deals that had earned an award for his team at Linklaters. He informed them that he had now set up his own law firm and that he was open for business. Many of them returned his emails, excited at the news. A couple agreed to meet him the following week. So he took the lift down from his office on the 12th floor to the 4th floor, where his friend Pak-Wo Shum ran Travel King, a travel agency. There, Elikem bought a ticket on credit to travel to London the following week to meet up with some of them and discuss possible alliances. The reception was refreshing, and incredibly different from his earlier experience back in Ghana.

"When I turned up at one of the law firms, Norton Rose Fulbright, nearly all the partners who did Africa work, together with the London managing partner, were present. They supported me and worked with me on a number of deals. It did not matter to them that my firm was a start-up or that I was relatively inexperienced, which was a stark contrast to my recent experience in Ghana. The partners saw my potential and did not look at me as a junior partner. In fact, one of the first few deals we handled was the sale of Ghana Telecom to Vodafone, which at the time was the second largest privatization in Ghana's history with an acquisition price of nearly a billion dollars for a 70% stake. The relationships I had built at Kellogg and in London played a big role at this point in time."

The Making of a Protégé

Elikem had always considered himself an entrepreneur and not just a lawyer. This perspective might have been cemented through his early experiences as a young lad, still tied to the apron strings of his parents. He fondly recalls how his father occasionally handled chieftaincy disputes, many of which he did pro bono. At Christmas, to show gratitude, the chiefs from the village would typically present bovine gifts to his father. Even at such a young age, Elikem had realized that the going rate for legal services had to be more than just a few heads of cattle or goats. He felt his father was too generous and should be focusing on top-paying clients.

"It irked me, and I determined to build a very different type of firm. We were going to focus only on corporate and high-net-worth clients, and we were going to build a profitable law firm from day one, which I achieved in the first month."

As Oxford & Beaumont grew, Elikem assembled some of the brightest young people in Ghana and had worked out his very own unique compensation plan. Since he was a stranger to the traditional echelons of many law firms (i.e., junior lawyer to associate, and up to senior partner), he had also managed to completely annihilate the hierarchical system in his firm.

"I practically threw all my employees into the pool, offered a little guidance and support, and allowed them to work out for themselves whether they would swim or drown."

He would meet one of his employees, who would eventually become a protégé (and later, a partner), in the most bizarre of circumstances. The chance encounter had in fact acted as an interview. While still at the bank, after a particularly stressful week, Elikem checked into an out-of-town destination spa. Hilary Komey, the hotel's marketing officer, had to be hauled in to address a situation. Elikem recalls that this was still back in the days when he was hot-headed and would throw a fit of outrage at the slightest inconvenience.

The hotel had messed up his reservations, and the room he had asked for was no longer available when he arrived. He had made quite a scene at the front desk, and with nostrils flaring, impatiently waited for the manager, whom he had demanded. He was eventually assuaged, not so much because the situation was resolved, but by the manner in which it was coolly handled. This would set the stage for their long working relationship.

Elikem found out that Hilary was an only child and did not enjoy living away from his mother who was back in Accra. He was therefore keen to get a job in Accra. During the course of that weekend, Elikem and Hilary hit it off. Armed with the information he had discovered about Hilary's personal circumstances, Elikem was keen to offer him a job at the law firm he was then planning in his head.

Elikem's only hesitation was that he had planned to implement in his new law firm a rule that restricted recruits only to university graduates. Hilary at the time had a diploma from a polytechnic, but not a university degree.

"I want you to come and work with me," Elikem announced as his eyes lit up in delight at the news. But then Hilary had to wait for the opportunity to come to fruition, which, luckily for him, was only a few months away. So when Oxford & Beaumont opened its doors for business, Hilary was the first hire.

"I hired Hilary on condition that he agreed to do a top-up course to convert his diploma into a degree. I was happy for him to start working for me part-time during the first year while he also attended university. He agreed and did not disappoint, bagging first-class honors in the process. On his graduation day, we splurged on a full-page ad on one of the local dailies with a message of congratulations celebrating his achievement. He also matured quickly and progressed through the ranks as the firm expanded, from my PA and office manager, to the business operations officer, then manager, and chief operations officer. After our merger (with ENSAfrica), he went on to become head of admin of our Cape Town office and is now practice integration manager (Africa-wide) within ENSAfrica."

When he first began to work with Hilary, there was a bit of frustration. He certainly had a lot of potential but had never worked at the level that Elikem expected. He had never been out of the country and had virtually no international exposure. As the team expanded, and right from day one, Elikem had always made it clear that Oxford & Beaumont was an international law firm, which just happened to be headquartered in Accra. Therefore, Elikem compelled him to tag along during his overseas trips and meetings, hoping for, at the very least, some exposure or even a cultural transplant of sorts.

During their first trip to London, Elikem turned to him in a jocular manner and said, "You know, I have brought you here so you can see how the teacups are arranged and how the lunch table is set during business meals so that you can do it properly when we get back home. Are we clear?"

"ENK," he replied, "I get what you are about."

Bingo! Elikem thought. They were on the same page. Elikem would later choose London as an incubator of sorts for his team, setting up an office there because he believed it was a market that easily provided the kind of exposure and mentality he was looking for. It became a rite of passage for his lawyers to spend months working in the London office just for the exposure and to build networks. It paid off as evidenced by the way the firm operated. More importantly for Elikem, it enabled him to build a firm that did not revolve around him as his lawyers gained access to the same London networks and acquired their own international exposure and experience.

In the period leading towards the end of 2008, Elikem recalls that the firm would have collapsed were it not for the fact that it could manage to run without his presence. The operations did not revolve around him, and when he could not work for a couple of months, everything went on smoothly.

"At the time, I worked too many hours. I was also teaching at the university and sat on three company boards, while at the same time I was writing my book. I had a mental breakdown that forced me into a recuperation break. When I returned, I realized that I did not like being stuck inside a law firm despite the fact that I had built it to its current staggering heights. Considering the state of my health, I hatched my own quiet exit strategy."

Oxford & Beaumont later merged with ENSAfrica, the largest law firm in Africa. Elikem now serves as a partner as well as Chairman of ENS Africa-Ghana and sits on the ENSAfrica board.

Thoughts about Tony

Tony Elumelu who is currently worth more than $700 million has been named (in 2012) one of Africa's 20 Most Powerful People by *Forbes* magazine. Elikem refers to Tony as "a dream merchant" due to the fact that he always harbors big audacious dreams for himself and encourages others—particularly the young—to dream as well.

"I have a lot of admiration for the man, considering where he has come from and where he is today. He trades in dreams, including other people's dreams. Tony fired up my dreams, and he continues to inspire many other Africans on a much larger scale through his foundation, The Tony Elumelu Foundation. He has a high disregard for the impossible. The fact that he is a massive extrovert has also helped his businesses to flourish because he loves people and relishes business socialization. When I met him, he was less interested in my academic credentials and job experience and more interested in who I was as a person. He was keen to administer the McKinsey test, 'Would I want to be stuck in an airport with this person?'"

The manner in which Tony Elumelu sold his dream to Elikem instantly reminded me of John Sculley and Steve Jobs back in the late 1980s. Steve Jobs had tried to lure John Sculley away from Pepsi into joining Apple. With Sculley on board, and with his solid business background and recent success at Pepsi, Apple would have a greater image of stability and success. At the end of the pitch, Steve Jobs posed the famous question to Sculley:

"Do you want to sell sugared water for the rest of your life, or do you want to come with me and change the world?"

The Learning Curve

I was eager to understand how Elikem felt about what I considered a steep learning curve when he returned to Ghana. Elikem notes that there was really not much he could do about his lack of experience. The first place he went to kick-start the learning curve was his MBA notes. He dug into his books all over again, including his notes on strategy and brand management. He also collected hundreds of case studies from all over the internet and picked out valuable tips. While abroad, he kept his networking channels warm. Therefore, his biannual visits to Ghana meant that he still had connections with a number of friends as well as business peers when he returned. He would later meet up with them for brainstorming sessions and to extract vital lessons from their experiences.

However, Elikem recalls that the most valuable class he ever took in business school was on organizational behavior.

"Whenever I speak to audiences today, I still use MBA jargon like *competitive advantage, long-term strategy, value proposition, balanced scorecard,* and *differentiation,* among others. But really when I peel the layers of the onion, I think we were able to achieve success because we relied on good old-fashioned values. The sort of simple things I learnt at the feet of my grandmother: respect for others, common sense, good manners, politeness, and courtesy. All these things are on the people side of the equation."

Other Subtle Influences on Doing Business in Africa

Back in the early days, and as the law firm grew, Elikem ran into what seemed like an insurmountable situation, one in which even the proverbial long arm of the law could not reach. Kwame, a budding Ghanaian entrepreneur and a good friend, waltzed into his office one morning. He had been trying to set up a business in a regulated industry and required approval from the relevant regulator. He was a dashing young man in his late twenties who had grown up in Ghana, but was frustrated by the turn of events. He had made endless trips to their offices, making his case for an approval for his business. But the officials tossed him about for several months, and he lost all hope.

During his innumerous trips to the offices, he had noticed that there were two parallel tracks that offered the same end product. He also learned, with a degree of sadness, that he had landed on the wrong track, the stagnant one that barely moved. The other path, which was much faster and more efficient, served the foreigners. After one of his many unfruitful trips, he settled down for lunch at a local joint, close to the arts center in Accra. Tourists usually thronged the arts center to purchase artifacts and souvenirs. Kwame then remembered that he was supposed to send some curios and other pieces of sculpture to some friends in the US. He wolfed down his lunch with renewed urgency and shuffled towards the arts center to procure the gifts for his friends.

"Hello," a nasal voice suddenly piped up next to him. He turned to look at the beaming Caucasian man who gestured towards the animal sculpture he was holding.

"Hello. How are you?"

"This is pretty nice, huh?"

Kwame turned, regarding the sculpture the older man held up for him to get a better view.

They launched into small talk and eventually ended up having a cup of coffee as soon as they were done with shopping. Kwame told him about himself, his business, and even the challenges he was facing before learning that the man was a volunteer and that he would be in the country for a few more months. Then an idea lit up in his young mind.

"I have been trying to get an approval for my business, and you won't believe it, but, from the look of things, it will be a cold day in hell before I get that approval," Kwame lamented after they had chatted up for about a quarter of an hour.

"Listen, why don't we go up together with you posing as a partner and then you can see what I mean. They won't give it to me because I am young and Ghanaian."

"And why is that?" the Caucasian said after catching his breath from a bout of laughter. "I would think it would be easier for a citizen than it would be for a foreigner," he wondered.

Relishing the adventure, the Caucasian agreed for his new friend to pose as a partner. They met up the next day near one of the bend-down boutiques in Kantamanto market in Accra, where Kwame procured a secondhand suit and shirt, after which they made a beeline for the regulator's offices. Within 3 days, they had received the required approval. It had taken the presence of an old, bald, pot-bellied, Caucasian man sitting confidently across the table and speaking the Queen's English.

Elikem reveals that he always tells this story to underscore the fact that despite all the education we have had in Africa, there remains a colonial mentality. He argues that "the best opportunities should be available to everyone."

Biggest Mistake

While he does not put much energy into regrets, Elikem notes that his biggest mistake would have to be how he managed his boss at the bank. If it were possible to push a rewind button, he would have handled things differently. As he reflects on his early days of management, he thinks the one thing he would have done is to have more humility.

"I think I was a little too hot-headed, given that I did not have a lot of experience."

Elikem remembers a particularly rebellious moment in his career. He had requested funds to have a consumer research agency carry out some research about the Ghanaian consumer so that they could design the bank's marketing strategies.

"I needed a clear understanding of the Ghanaian banking consumer, and the fact that I had never even held a Ghanaian bank account did not help the situation. My request was turned down, and the reason given was that there were already many employees who had experience and they would give their input."

In what he now considers to have been a degree of hubris, he set out anyway and hired two fresh-faced university students with whom he scoured the length and breadth of Ghana, collecting raw data from the consumers. They went to churches, markets, schools, bus parks, and practically anywhere, they could find a large number of people to interview. In just 2 weeks, they had collected a rich set of data.

"After the 2 weeks that I spent out in the streets and marketplaces, I knew more about banking in Ghana than anyone else in the firm."

The strategy he crafted later on would rely heavily on the data he had collected. He wrote such an insightful report that even the MD grudgingly refunded him his research expenses. Elikem concedes that he seemed to be permanently on eye-gouging terms with the MD, which might have been avoided at no cost to either of them. Looking back, his strained relationship with the MD might have been a consequence of his immaturity at the time and his overly emotional stance on issues. He could have tried to better understand the situations and compromise whenever possible in order to achieve more.

"Regrets," he notes, quoting an African proverb, "are very much like grandchildren; they come much later on."

Elikem credits that professional period with the leadership style he developed, which was key in helping to grow his law firm. Based on his own experience where he felt stifled and frustrated, Elikem focuses on an open culture where there are no sacred cows other than the firm's values and mission. "Everything else is potentially up for debate." His leadership philosophy is "leadership by listening and management by debate." He encourages healthy discussions and fosters an environment of transparency.

Takeaway:

- Africa is home to a vast pool of young talent in need of training and education.
- When building networks, also consider reaching outside of Africa to advance a business agenda.

Chapter XIV

A taste of Success with Coca-Cola in Africa

Prosper Tchouambé and Charles "Charly" Elamé were sitting on the Tarco Airways' Yakovlev Yak-42 en route to Hargeisa, Somaliland. The all-metal, low-winged, 120-seat, three-engine aircraft was the brainchild of Alexander Sergeyevich Yakovlev. The Soviet aeronautical engineer turned politician later in his career developed some of the best warplanes of the Soviet Air Force during World War II. The Yak-42 was one of only two commercial airlines Yakovlev's Design Bureau ever built.

The two Coca-Cola executives were actually on their way back to Nairobi, and Hargeisa was a stopover for a couple of days. The flight from Djibouti to Hargeisa, a one-hour commute, had initiated its descent when the plane entered a violent turbulence zone midair. Turbulence was a common occurrence in the area as the enclave is located on the coastline and bears a mountainous and rugged terrain. Besides, the plane was flying against strong, westbound, gale-force winds from tropical monsoons. Prosper's eyes met the hostess's, and the young Sudanese woman offered a comforting smile. Unbeknownst to her, Prosper was actually quite familiar with bouncing airplanes and trips to remote lands in Africa. With his Commercial Manager, he was heading to the horn of Africa's breakaway state.

In 1960, the British Somaliland and Italian Somaliland gained their independence and merged into a single country, Somalia. Thirty-one years later, the former British protectorate split again from Somalia and unilaterally declared its independence following the ousting of Somali President Major General Mohamed Siad Barre. The move threw the country into chaos and civil war, which ensues to this day. Although Somalia has attracted unwanted international attention with piracy off its coast, largely publicized by blockbuster movies like Paul Greengrass' *Captain Phillips* featuring Tom Hanks and Somali-American actor Barkhad Abdi, Somaliland—a country not recognized by the international community—had been stable, in comparison to the war-torn south. For the umpteenth time, Prosper ran through his mental checklist of challenges for their project he expected once they arrived in the country: water scarcity, tribal enmities, inexistent distribution routes, etc. While he was deep in thought 10,000 feet above ground, on the tarmac in Hargeisa, their local would-be partner was waiting for them, flanked by bodyguards toting AK-47s.

A Career with the Coca-Cola Company

Prosper spent 25 years working for the Coca-Cola Company, during which time he visited close to 70 countries, relocating 11 times and in places like Manila, Bangkok, Casablanca, Nairobi, Douala, Dakar, Abidjan, and Lagos. He spent his last 10 years at Coca-Cola as General Manager in charge of 22 countries in the Indian Ocean and Africa.

Prosper is a hard-hitting person prompt to take an unwavering stand behind his convictions. *Challenge, deliver, commitment, double-digit growth, opportunity, no excuses* are all words and phrases that frequently pop up in his conversations.

Prosper was born and brought up in Cameroon, where he undertook his early education, both tertiary and secondary. He later went to France to study architecture, where he graduated one year before his class. While he did not expressly relay it to me, the early steps towards management may have been more exploratory than tactical. Soon after, he was off to study finance in the US before finally landing in the Georgia Tech School of Management in Atlanta, where he completed a Master's in Business Administration. It was then that he joined Coca-Cola, fresh out of management school, and was immediately posted to

Manila, the bayside capital city of the Philippines for what would become a decades' long career with the company embodying best what corporate America is.

Prosper is incredibly upbeat about the continent's prospects. Given the depth of his experience in Africa, one would hardly dispute his perspective. In fact, I had barely finished my question about his general views of the continent before he nearly cut me off, prognosticating on the outcomes for the next 5 years.

"Over a space or period of time—5 to 6 years—you will have a lot of opportunities to do business in Africa, mainly in the space of FMCG, and mainly in the space of packaged goods. In Africa, a lot of the important things are in place. There may be a host of issues in Africa, such as disease outbreaks, social and political instability, harsh weather conditions, and so on, but when you are dedicated to the market, you are able to succeed in spite of those issues."

He is quick to add that the kind of commercial success such as the one Coca-Cola has enjoyed boils down to a single word—*discipline*. It is about perseverance, and being a perennial optimist about the market. While everything might seem up for grabs for a large multinational conglomerate, the likes of Coca-Cola, one has to stay the course. Only then can a coup d'état or a drought no longer become an obstacle for meeting targets. Discipline is at the core of Coca-Cola's success in Africa, to the point that some have quipped that one may have an easier access to a liter of soda than a liter of clean water in the continent. According to Prosper, passion and long-term, unwavering dedication to the market is critical.

"During my tenure as General Manager for West and Central Africa, we grew the EBITDA twofold from 30 to 62 million US dollars over a period of 4 years." According to Prosper, five success factors, at the core of Coca-Cola's success in Africa, could be replicated by any global company operating in Africa.

Success Factor 1: Commitment to the Continent

"Beside the fact that it has a strong and global brand, Coca-Cola is really committed to the continent and has bet on African talents to chart the future of the company. At the beginning of 2000, we were given the latitude, within a framework, to capture opportunities that have been elusive. The company had to change its paradigm on Africa. It needed people who understood and had a stake in the continent. People who could take the transformative power of the brands and create opportunities for communities across the continent. An example of such commitment was a mission we took to set up the first bottling operation in Hargeisa, Somaliland, where a local entrepreneur has been trying for over 10 years to set up a bottling factory. The initial purpose of the trip was to meet the future partner, size up the opportunity, and the economic impact on the community. Water availability is an issue in the Somaliland desert, and if we were going to grant a franchise, we had to ensure that this was not going to adversely affect the community.

We flew in from Djibouti and were met at the airport by our partner. He was from a prominent local tribe and guaranteed our safety during our stay. We drove to our hotel and to the Hargeisa Water Agency to understand the water challenge. To size up the place we drove all the way to the border with Puntland and then to the port of Berbera. Despite the raging conflicts in Somalia, Somaliland was a haven—a relative peace where business was thriving. Beyond the economic benefit of a Coca-Cola factory, they also believe it could give additional credibility to their bid to be an independent, sovereign country."

Success Factor 2: Build Strong Business Ethics and Values

"Many emerging countries in Africa are working hard to curb corruption. Companies' associates in these countries are constantly exposed to unwarranted practices. For a global company, this presents a major risk. The DNA of any successful company is made up of a strong code of ethics that is constantly refreshed to employees, to partners, and to key stakeholders. Integrity is critical in an environment that could be very demanding on a personal level and where opportunities for shortcuts are many. Lack of integrity of the leadership and team members will compromise any ability to deliver sustained performance.

At Coca-Cola, the company leaders were given the latitude and adequate resources to address the challenge and the opportunities of their time in the position. A decision to expand—or not—the footprint of the company is left to the local management unit. The company sets overall business principles that give freedom within a framework to associates around the world.

To entertain a government official or a manager of a publicly owned company for lunch, for instance, an authorization from the headquarters in Atlanta is required.

Any gift of more than 25 dollars USD needed special approvals. We had several ways to ensure that the culture was entrenched. Every six months we had a pulse employee engagement survey. In a continent like Africa, this actually makes your life as a manager very easy as these rules are communicated broadly to the larger community. We never received any solicitations, as we made sure that our values were known. The leadership embodied the values rather than preaching them."

Success Factor 3: Visualize the Opportunity, Focus on the Prize

"Africa could indeed be challenging, and therefore you will always have a room full of people who have failed and are ready to discourage you, even reciting Ecclesiastes 1:9, to claim there is nothing new under the sun. You can ignore them. The opportunities are real.

I remember that the team initially did not believe the targets we set were achievable. They had tried many ideas over the past 10 years. The same mind-set prevailed at the bottler, and not many gave us much of a chance when they saw us bringing up stretched targets. The plan was first to ensure the team members' buy-in, so we set out to spend time in the field, out in the streets of Dakar, Cotonou, Abidjan, and explore the opportunities with the creation of new transaction points. Our investigations and analysis of the market led to the formulation of our strategy: to capture the opportunities, we had to adjust the pricing of the single serve and build a last mile in terms of cold chain infrastructure to the informal sector traders. This would double their income and create employment for millions of people of in the continent. The consumption benchmarks with similar markets such as Nairobi, Bangkok, and Manila also helped structure the discussion with the team.

Once the team was sold to the concept and convinced of the opportunities, we took the sales pitch to the independent franchise bottlers. The bottler makes the capital investment, and as such, they needed a solid case to move in our direction. We were basically internal consultants to the system. It took us 6 months of constantly breaking down the opportunity stories in various forms and shapes to convince the bottler in Paris that we could increase profits. The case is made simple with the understanding that a significant increase in the number of transactions would inevitably grow the gross margin. If you have excess capacity, by reducing the retail price you could create a velocity that can help generate more revenue, gain share, and potentially create the right social impact. Until then, the typical way to increase profit was an annual price increase. However, the increased competition in the industry made this strategy difficult. As the leader in the industry, we needed to get an edge with efficiency and drive new transactions.

The lesson here is to accept that people might not be seeing the opportunities you are seeing. In the end, we achieved in West Africa everything we set out to do from the beginning. Double digit profit in 4 years, launch a profitable juice business, and build a strong team."

Success Factor 4: Empower the Local Team

"When the direction is set and clear, it is necessary to empower the local team. At Coca-Cola, senior local managers have employment contracts limited to 3 years. With a 3-year-only employment contract in hand, one quickly learns that to have an impact it is imperative to empower the local team. Not only one's direct team but also all those in the value chain down to the final delivery of product or service. Coca-Cola's freedom-within-the-framework only defined the broad boundaries of our actions. The company contracts the targets and resources with a manager and his team; and the rest is left to her and her team. The constraint allows for local innovation and produces the best from the team. The ability to lead from the back then becomes critical. Once the team is aligned on the opportunities and is given the training and the resources to implement the strategies, one has to now stand back to allow them to create their own war stories, their own private victories. The Coke Zero success in West Africa was a good example of this success factor. For the company, the new drink was a lifestyle beverage that sold at premium. The marketing team spotted a bigger opportunity with health-conscious older consumers beyond the cities. They came up with a very successful program to reach that population. We sold it at parity with the other brands and positioned the drink with population above 40. Coke Zero is a major success for Coca-Cola in Africa to this day. The team challenged the company to propose positioning and gave the latitude to experiment, based on its own hypotheses and market realities."

Success Factor 5: Planning against All Odds

"Once the plan is agreed to, one has to deliver, no matter what happens in the market that is outside one's control.

The first day I took over the region, the first crisis I had to deal with was the civil war in Côte d'Ivoire. The crisis had reached a point where we needed to airlift the whole staff out of Abidjan. I was still based in Lagos, and I overheard in a restaurant a security company manager with an office in Abidjan discussing moving of expats from their home to the airport. We connected with our office in Abidjan. Next we found a jet that would fly in Abidjan during the night and exfiltrate our employees and their families to Cotonou. The first meeting I had with the team was in a small guest house in Cotonou. We discussed their individual situations, the commitment of the company to their safety and that of their families. During that meeting, we decided to relocate part of the team to another location. We split the team between Dakar and Abidjan for one year. I had big plans and double-digit growth targets and a revenue growth strategy to sell and execute.

In many American companies, what matters most is not the base profit but the incremental profit year on year. This is paramount when the company is a listed company. In Africa many companies are just happy to simply turn a profit. These companies are generally privately owned. In an American company in general and Coca-Cola in particular, the culture is to deliver the target weekly, monthly, and quarterly. The discipline is brutal. It is even more challenging as a blow-up will always happen in Africa.

Planning for performance becomes a refined game whereby one has to develop her own algorithm and constantly build scenarios. Our position was to work simultaneously on a pipeline of short-term, medium-term, and long-term (18 months, the time to build a new plant) projects and marketing initiatives, to prioritize high leverage initiatives with major impact, and to constantly look for new opportunities to feed the pipelines and hedge against market risk."

A Coca-Cola Plant in the Desert

In May 2012, Coca-Cola opened a 15-million-dollar USD state-of-the-art bottling plant an hour's drive from Hargeisa, the first major industrial investment of its kind in the territory. Somaliland Beverage Industry created 100 direct jobs and 2,500 indirect jobs. The SBI plant churns out approximately 11,000 bottles of soft drinks every hour. The project also paved the way to other social initiatives such as the provision of clean water to 50,000 displaced people in Somaliland. With Coca-Cola's move in Somaliland, only two countries remain without a Coca-Cola franchise: North

Korea and Cuba.

Takeaway:

- The company passion and dedication to the market can help compensate for some of the shortcomings in the market on occasion.

- Africa is a continent of tremendous opportunity for FCMG companies willing to leverage local talents and adopt a local approach to doing business.

Chapter XV

Growing a Taste for Fresh African Juices

François' heart was about to explode out of his chest. He was sitting alone in his company car, a massive Toyota Land Cruiser branded on each front door with the letters, "U" and "N" in bold with the engine revving. Everything seemed so unreal, so Hollywood, like the entire moment was pulled out of some blockbuster movie. Lately, he had been driving most of the time with the windows down to avoid inhaling the foul smell released from what increasingly resembled litter on the car floor: empty packs of chips and soda cans, remains of street food that his family had fed on during this long and perilous journey from Kigali to the southwest border near Bukavu. Cleaning it up had been the last of his concerns since they hurriedly left their cozy home in Kigali, out of fear of all getting killed by militias.

The engine was still revving. Outside, the moisture-laden air from the previous day's heavy and persistent rainfall made it difficult to breathe. He was so nervous he could hardly feel his fingernails digging through his sweaty palms as he clutched hard on the wheels of his 4x4. He tried to stay as calm as he could, but with all his senses in alert. Everything had happened so fast over the past few months for the International Trade Centre's (ITC, a United Nations body for trade-related technical assistance) Director for Rwanda. For a minute, he thought this was his lucky day. The officer who first checked his papers was not familiar with official documents and did not notice that the papers were actually doctored. He had made them up himself to cross the border and save his life. However, as his papers were turned over to another senior-ranking officer, the deception was about to be exposed and he was wondering whether this was not instead his last day on earth.

It was in the early hours of the morning on May 27, 1994. The genocide in Rwanda was raging in the cities and in the countryside. François has spent the past several weeks playing hide and seek with fate. He knew from one of his neighbors in Kigali that his name was now on the list of people to kill, and there would not be another occasion if he could not escape here, at the border between Rwanda and Zaire[1].

The telephone rang in the shack that was used by the soldiers as a frontier station. François opened his ears and focused hard to listen to the conversation. And then he overheard his name in the middle of the conversation in

---

[1] Today the Democratic Republic of Congo (DRC)

French.

"Vous avez dit Soma? François Soma? Oui, il est actuellement ici avec nous au poste frontière et...[1]"

And then, a loud noise tore in the air outside. The officer threw the handset and ran outside. The wooden barrier had been shattered by the 4x4 and François was racing full throttle for his life towards the Zairian border crossing. The car dashed across the small bridge on the 117-kilometer-long Ruzisi river, which served as a natural frontier between Rwanda and Zaire and only stopped several hundred meters further down the path when the Zairian border patrol pointed their guns at him. When he finally turned the engine of his Land Cruiser off, he sighed and recited one single prayer: The prayer to God was not a thanks for saving his life. No. His life was saved, indeed, and he was a million times grateful for it, but God's job was just not done yet in his mind: his wife, his son, and two daughters were still on the other side of the border, on Rwandan soil, and he desperately needed another miracle.

A Love Story with Switzerland

After his escape from Rwanda, François returned to

---

[1] Dis you say Soma? François Soma? Yes, he is right now here with us at the border and...

Switzerland where he had, years before, acquired his master's in marketing at the Haute Etudes Commerciales at the Université de Lausanne. He spent the following 20 years working as a consultant for ITC, mainly in Africa. His years of experience helped him build a solid understanding of the intricacies of doing business in Africa, and he developed a multidisciplinary network of businesspeople in the continent. When François retired in 2016, he started his own company and put to practice his vast experience in the private sector in Africa in his adopted village of Bussigny-près-Lausanne in Switzerland with the same idea he had been pushing during his time at ITC: export from Africa to developed markets. BSI Import-Export Services SARL was launched and François started scouting for the best suppliers to provide him with quality fruit juice from African farms.

Exporting Mangoes to Europe

"You know, Ben, we have achieved certain outcomes at ITC for which I am pretty proud. In 2006, Mali had an issue exporting their considerable stock of mangoes. The government was trying to diversify from cotton, livestock, and gold. Mango was considered an interesting area to develop in this view. They turned to ITC to assist them in the process and find avenues to export their mango crops. You know Mali very well, and during the harvest season, you only have to bend down to get a handful of fresh, beautiful, and juicy mangoes. They cost almost nothing and can be found everywhere, from Bamako to the border with Burkina Faso. Associations of mango producers were bogged with the question of finding international markets for their products. The ITC bureau was tasked with finding a solution to this problem. I went to Bamako the first time to meet with the business community involved in mango production.[1] They were flooding the local market. A few businesspeople from France had contacted them to make an attempt at exporting to France, only to realize that they were actually being grudged."

Mali is a landlocked country in West Africa, and the Malians would sell their mangoes to businessmen and ship containers of fruits to France through the Autonomous Port of Abidjan in Côte d'Ivoire. Six to eight months later, the businessmen would return to Mali and tell their local partners that they could not sell the products as expected. Indeed, there was always an excuse for not paying in full for the fruit containers that were exported. Damaged goods, goods arriving after the season was over so prices were low,

---

[1] Bamako is the capital of Mali

crops affected by anthracnose, etc. The Malian exporters would then find themselves cornered into accepting whatever payment was thrown at them for their products. On contacting the ITC, they were eager to find a way out, or at least a fairer compensation for their yields.

François invited them to Fruit Logistica, a produce trade show, in Berlin in 2008. The exhibition was celebrating its 15th anniversary the first time Mali attended. Two years prior, Fruit Logistica had introduced FLIA (FRUIT LOGISTICA Innovation Award) to "recognize outstanding innovations in the entire fresh produce supply chain, ranging from production all the way to point of sale." The award was won by Rijk Zwaan, a Netherlands-based vegetable-breeding company for their new type of lettuce.

The fruit exhibition gave Mali the international platform it was looking for to meet with a variety of business partners ready to import and sell their mangoes in their own markets, and help them develop harvests that would comply with international standards.

"The ITC booked a stand for Mali at the exhibition, with sparkles, the national flag, and all the fanfare. We took pictures, and created tremendous exposure for the country to showcase their fruits. We came back 4 years in a row to present Malian mangoes. Soon enough, Germans, Belgians, and other European customers were showing interest in the

Malian products, and contact details were exchanged."

When François returned to Mali a few years later, the response from several of his friends from the Mango Associations in the country—AMELEF [1] and APEFEL—were very satisfied with the outcomes of the ITC initiative. Satisfaction may be relative, but it was a significant start. Despite production estimated at 600,000 tons per year by the World Bank, Mali exports today only about 6 percent of these volumes. A lot more remains to be done by all the organizations on the ground to support the sector.

Interestingly, François notes that the Mali example inspired their colleagues from the Tanzanian Association of Mango Growers (AMAGRO) who were facing similar issues exporting their products to international markets. François, who is fluent in Swahili, the national language in Tanzania, brought five Tanzanian delegates to Mali to learn from the Malian experience with ITC and other support agencies.

"If you take the example of Mali, I believe that one of the biggest issues they faced was the lack of control of the value chain. For Tanzania, they had issues with the quality of the export product. European or North American markets

---

[1] Association Malienne des Exportateurs de Fruits et Légumes, or *Malian Association of Fruits and Vegetables Exporters* and Association Professionnelle des Exportateurs de Fruits et Légumes, or Professional Association of Fruits and Vegetables Exporters

prefer certain types of mangoes, and it was important to have a strong knowledge of these subtleties."

Doing It Myself

His experience at ITC left François somewhat frustrated. The feeling that more could have been done to support local exports from Africa lingered.

"I was fairly comfortable and making a decent income from my job. But then I asked myself, what did I achieve over these decades promoting exports from Africa? It is true that I met a lot of people in the private sector, made hundreds of presentations, and displayed statistics. But ultimately, there was a lot of unfinished business. I felt that I could take advantage of my retirement to carry on at a personal level this ambition of exporting quality products from Africa that meet international requirements."

François elected to import in Switzerland pineapple and ginger juice from Benin. He partnered with a local food engineer who produced the juice. François made a trip to Morocco to select the packaging and then print the labels in Switzerland.

François pulls a few samples from a paper bag he brought with him, and hands them over to me for tasting. I am a huge ginger juice fan and open that bottle first. I am slightly surprised that François opted for a glass bottle as a container for his products, as paperboard packs and plastic containers are more commonly used these days for this type of product. François notes that plastic and metal containers may interact with the taste of the food, while paper containers are fragile. The choice of glass, although a lot heavier, came quite naturally.

The Distribution Challenge

If François readily acknowledges that he possesses a great deal of expertise with the intricacies of an import-export business, he is only now learning the ropes when it comes to distribution. He shipped a full container of pineapple and ginger juices from his supplier in Benin. He rented out a warehouse 100 meters away from his house and contracted two salespeople to help him sell his products to restaurants, hotels, corner shops, and directly to consumers.

François hired salespeople from Africa, whom he believed would be culturally connected to his product and African communities. Although he was eager to introduce his juices to Western consumers, he also considered African communities in Europe as a low-hanging fruit. In Africa, drinking homemade ginger or pineapple juice is almost as popular and common as drinking Coca-Cola. Therefore, he would not need to work hard to launch his drinks in these communities. But the Western consumer was definitely his ideal target group. On one hand, this constituted a completely exotic product for them; and on the other hand, they were better suited financially to buy his drinks. He also considered it a challenge that African consumers in Europe had access to all of the ingredients required to make pineapple or ginger juices in their homes.

Business Procrastination

A problem that François faced early on was the "Bio" certification label for his juices. The growing trend in Western markets is to sell products labeled as "Bio." The requirement was not mandatory from the regulatory body, but was necessary to reach a clientele that was increasingly environmentally conscious. François saw the label as a plus that would increase the appeal of his products. He knew an institute in Switzerland that specialized in "Bio" certification, Ecocert. A date was set for the inspection of the production facility in Cotonou, and Ecocert dispatched an expert from its Ouagadougou office, Burkina-Faso to Benin.

When the expert reached Cotonou, François was flabbergasted to discover that his supplier was nowhere to be found. He tried to reach him over the phone, given the critical nature of the matter, to ensure that the expert from Ecocert was attended to so he could validate the Bio certification. Besides, François was paying for the expert's stay in Cotonou, and the longer the delay before he could proceed with the certification, the larger the bill he would have to pay to Ecocert.

"I still don't understand. I spent 3 days trying to get hold of him, and you would not believe where he was. While we had been planning for this certification for months already, he decided to attend funerals in Abomey. I know that no one can anticipate such a sad event, but at least you can appoint someone, find an alternative solution, or even request a postponement of the certification visit. The sentiment is that he did not necessarily perceive time as a critical element for his business. The prospect of accessing new markets and export in greater volumes was less important and not a priority in the face of the funerals."

I smiled. I could understand François' disappointment. I remembered once during a trip to Africa, after showing my frustration at someone being late to an appointed meeting, a man told me, "The White man may have invented the watch, but in Africa, time belongs to us."

Escape from Rwanda – Part II

An older friend during my teenaged years told me once that he had a simple, two-rule technique for decision making. It all had to do with gauging the options on the table. ("There are always several options," he used to say, "even when it looks otherwise.") For decisions affecting the short term, he goes with the lesser of two evils. For long-term impact decisions, he never picks options that were irrevocable and looked like one-way tickets. Throughout the years, I considered this advice to be some of the best I ever heard. Listening to François recounting his escape from Rwanda and how he managed to survive all along the journey, I had the deep feeling that he had either a better decision-making technique, or a very special guardian angel looking after him.

Exactly two weeks after crossing the Zaire border, François successfully organized the rescue of all his family. With the help of one of his dedicated friends and the ITC, he brought his family to Bukavu. At 2 a.m. on June 9, 1994, they quietly crossed Lake Kivu's wetlands on a dugout canoe to reunite with him. The ITC then supported the family relocation to Switzerland. They all live happily today in the canton of Vaud.

Takeaway:

- Investing time into understanding the priorities of local associates—sometimes rooted in tradition—could help avoid a dispute.
- Opening local productions—agricultural or industrial—is a priority for African nations in search of diversification from natural resources.

Chapter XVI

An Entrepreneurship Journey and a 7-year Detour

Elizabeth's trip to Westgate Mall always managed to elicit a fresh wave of dolefulness. Thin slices of forlorn memories of her now failed retail business would waft into her mind unfettered every time she walked through the mall's corridors. A tinge of woeful reminiscence welled up within her, albeit to a lesser degree with every subsequent visit, but with remarkable consistency nonetheless. The glory days of her business were now buried within Westgate Mall, which now served as a marker, a memory of what might have been a flourishing retail business. One of her recently closed shops had been located at Westgate Mall, a prominent shopping centre by any Nairobi standards.

Because of the proximity of the mall to her residence and, perhaps from sheer force of habit, an occasional visit to the mall was almost inevitable. Nevertheless, on this particular Saturday, she was in and out of the mall in a whoosh, this time managing to quell a faint stir of memory for her failed retail business as she drove to her next errand. When she arrived home later that afternoon, the 21st of

September 2013, she was jolted out of her reminiscence by the screaming global headlines. A group of Al-Shabab militants had attacked Westgate Mall just a few hours after she had left, killing nearly 100 innocent shoppers and shop owners, and holding a good number of shoppers hostage for hours.

Born To Be an Entrepreneur

Elizabeth always knew she wanted to be an entrepreneur. Her father had been in the hospitality industry while her mother had built a successful retail business. He went right into managing his own business in the hotel and hospitality industry as soon as he graduated. He would enter into a management contract with the owners of a facility and either earn his pay after he had met certain targets, or keep the operational profits after paying them a monthly contractual fee. Right from kindergarten, Elizabeth grew up knowing that her parents did not have the 8-5 kind of jobs that her friends' parents had.

They were entrepreneurs and she had never known them to ever be employed.

"They took us to school every day and I knew right from

back then that it wanted to be self-employed. This was very unique at the time. For the 70's and the 80's, my parents had a smaller family size. They were both educated and believed in family planning. They also made it clear that the minimum education expected from any of their children was a university degree."

There were alternative role models, Elizabeth's uncles and aunties had admirable, stable, steady income generating 8-5 jobs. She knew this because they led relatively good lives and seemed comfortable. That should have prompted, at the very least, her curiosity if not interest in their jobs or careers at a time when her own identity and path was still hazy and bit unclear. However, Elizabeth was attracted to her parents' career path. It felt like a prodding behind her back, urging her towards entrepreneurship. "I always knew that I wanted to be like my mum and my dad. They were the role models I had grown up observing. My uncles and aunties had 8-5 jobs which worked out quite well for them. But somehow, I was attracted more to my parents' career paths.

I'd always admired that the fact that they always had control over many elements of their lives and their work in general. This is because they were self-employed and so I definitely wanted that for myself as well."

Her penchant for independence grew from her early

days, and she seemed to get off to a good start. Her good grades in school worked out in her favour, and she had a bit of wiggle room at university. She had a wide array of courses to choose from due to her excellent grades. A school teacher once asked her what she would you like to do with herself? Her emphatic answer? "I want to be an entrepreneur," she announced with rehearsed but unmistakable resolution.

The teacher was clearly thrown by her declaration. She reevaluated her analysis and settled on architecture, which was then the only career she knew that would guarantee self-employment.

"If you want to be self-employed," she recommended, "then you'll have to choose architecture. That way, you can set up your own company and work independently," she advised in an uncertain tone. The very word *entrepreneur* was still alien in the academic hallways, and certainly not part of the lexicon of a fully-fledged career path. Therefore, architecture seemed like the closest career option if you were looking to run your own show.

This was not exactly a bull's eye in terms of what she had in mind as a career choice, but it was close enough. At least it guaranteed some form of independence and some semblance of the entrepreneur life she'd seen and admired at home. She broke the news to her eager parents during the vacation, and a year and a half later, she was shipped off to architectural school for her first year. This was the beginning of her career journey, which, at any rate, had promised independence. However, by the second week of her first year, she came to a sudden and disconcerting realization that she'd travelled hundreds of miles on the wrong road. What's more, the first opportunity for a U-turn was still hundreds of miles away.

"On the first day of class for the second week of my first year, it finally dawned on me as I sat in the class that I should have taken a Bachelor of Commerce instead or any other economics-oriented course. That would have been more useful to me given that I wanted to go straight into business after completing my university studies. I was now stuck with architecture and had to go through with it."

Elizabeth recalls that the education system at the time was anything but flexible. Everything seemed to be cast in stone and not as advanced as it is now. If she were to as much as consider switching courses, she would have to resign from her course and stay home for at least 3 years before finally returning to begin a new course. But this was not even the biggest problem.

Architectural courses were some of the most prestigious university courses to take, right up there with medicine and law. The biggest challenge was, how could she look her father in the face, after she had declared the course to be her choice, and inform him that she was going to stay home as a form four certificate holder for 3 years? It was out of the question. She elected to forge on with her architectural degree, more resignedly than resolutely.

In the second year of her studies, Elizabeth joined the Rotaract Club where she met Arjun Rijhwani, an astute engineer and businessman of Asian origin. He took her under his wing, mentored her, and even introduced her to a lot of his cronies who were in the leadership development space. But more importantly, Arjun helped her to realize that a degree was just paper and that it did not dictate what she could eventually do with her life. Elizabeth finally graduated from the University of Nairobi with an architectural degree, which was a prestigious accolade at the time.

"One day Arjun stopped me and said, 'Listen, this is just a piece of paper. It is not a lifetime contract that will force you to follow that particular career path.' Knowing that was freeing."

Post University

When she rolled out of university, Elizabeth naturally went down the path of looking for a job, which wasn't easy to come by. She had contributed to her university cost by taking on short-term engagements in team building, leadership development, and even media relations for organizations like Outward Bound, the National Leadership School, and Alliance Group Hotels. She was also a volunteer programme officer at Uvumbuzi–a membership society focused on environmental conservation. This experience enabled her to secure a job, first as an intern financial analyst and ICDC Investment (now Centum) and later as a Finance and Administration Manager at Nature Kenya. In her year at Nature Kenya she was involved in the development of the strategic plan for the organisation and during that process she wrote her job out of the organisational structure. She was back on the job market.

While she looked for a new opportunity she ran team building and leadership development programmes on a consultancy basis for companies such as Barclays Bank of Kenya and Shell-BP. The companies she was working with at the time suggested that she should set up a private limited company so that they could directly contract her on short-term projects on an as-needed basis.

"It was an excellent idea, and I registered a limited liability company in 2002. I was young and energetic, and it never once occurred to me that I was now pitting myself against heavyweights in the consulting industry such as PricewaterhouseCoopers and Deloitte. They would, most assuredly, crush me with the sheer force of their weight if we ever competed for the same assignment."

This thrilled as well as scared Elizabeth and her fledgling consultancy outfit, which had already begun to run into the usual start-up problems that plague entrepreneurs. Even after years of inspiration and watching others successfully run their businesses, she realized that she was not an expert at managing a business.

"I had an office space with five very expensive employees, but I was not good in financial management. I was also not good in people management at that point in time. It was a painstaking two and a half years before my consulting company finally folded. I never went to business school, but those early mistakes became my diploma on how to run a business."

Later on, Elizabeth stumbled on the idea of being an independent consultant, a slight variation of her former setup. She started out with team building, soft skills training and capacity building projects but over time dropped them for being labour-intensive. She now focuses on facilitation and moderation, helping teams develop strategies, plans, and providing expertise on organizational development. That had been the foundation of her transformative journey as far as her work is concerned and one which she suspects will continue to evolve.

In 2007, she took a stab at the retail space. There was a fast-growing middle-class population in the Kenyan capital, and retail was vibrant and growing in leaps. With the surplus income from her consultancy business, she set up her first retail shop.

"My costs for the consultancy business were relatively low. So I thought, why not start a business and try to diversify as well as multiply my sources of income? So I set up a retail shop in Prestige Plaza, one of the nice new retail malls in the capital. I was doing children's clothes and toys and early play-learning materials."

A new mall, the Westgate Mall, opened up in 2009, where she also managed to secure some space to expand her business. She was now running two retail outlets in Nairobi, unaware that she had just enrolled for an advanced business lesson. The business showed a lot of promise, but Elizabeth had neither envisioned nor carefully thought out how the rent models for such retail businesses worked out. What's more, she had to not only run the business, but also perform the uphill task of building her own supply chain from the ground up.

In retrospect, Elizabeth believes that if she only had to focus on building the business, she might have had some success. But she had to also build a working supply chain as well as secure business financing. Her mother had been in the retail business, and would occasionally share trinkets of advice on the ins and outs of her business. Despite this support, Elizabeth discovered that she never did really grasp the clockwork of the retail business, especially at the scale that she had ventured into. The business was soon on life support, and the bills were piling up. She had to pull the plug.

"There was a demand for the products, but the local manufacturers did not focus on my line. I had to source and set up arrangements with external manufacturers in order to stock the products. The local manufacturing industry as a whole had focused on FMCGs. All of a sudden, I was the importer, distributor, retailer, and even the one doing the warehousing. One day I did the calculations on the back of a used envelope and realized that it would be a cold day in hell before I broke even."

Finally coming to the logical conclusion, she closed both

shops in 2010. It was a sad affair, and for the next few weeks, she sat back and reflected on the outcome of her retail business. She was jolted out of her melancholy by the screaming news headlines. There was a terrorism incident at the mall where one of her shops had been located. If she had been in the mall, she would most probably have been caught up in the terrorism attack where more than 100 people lost their lives. It was a gruesome incident that made worldwide headlines.

"Al-Shabab, the infamous, notorious, Somali-based insurgent group had launched an ambush on Kenya, targeting the Westgate Mall and killing shoppers and shop owners as retaliation for Kenya's alleged interference in their country's affairs. For sure, that's where I would have been, together with my son, who was just 3 year old."

Rather than a failure, Elizabeth considers her business venture to be a pricey diploma on how to run a business. The occasional discovery of gems within the world of commerce, however small, will always lure entrepreneurs back to the digging, however grand their earlier failures. Elizabeth is already working on developing an idea on job creation into a business venture. One of the important lessons she picked up was the fact that one should not start or run a business on their own. She is in the process of building relationships and finding partners who can act as a sounding board for business development as well as "make up" for her many shortcomings.

Doing Business in Africa

Elizabeth considers doing business in Africa to be mostly a story of resilience. Even in her current work as a management and process consultant, resilience is, in most cases, the consistent underlying factor. But then one needs to directly go through the experience. However simple and seemingly insignificant, experience eventually counts and adds to the bigger picture of how one understands the continent.

One time during a work trip with a colleague, Elizabeth nearly scoffed when the colleague made it known that she wanted a particular kind of room when they checked into the hotel in Benin. Top on her list was a hot water shower, more or less a standard in many hotels. But Elizabeth opted to stay mum and let her colleague experience the surprise all by herself. In Benin—and the Sahel— you will almost never need to take a hot water shower. The heat already heats up the water by the time it comes out of the tap. Her colleague never once turned on the hot water shower.

One of the most challenging projects she has worked on involved the improvement of productivity of smallholder farmers, enabling them to commercialize their production in three different regions of Kenya. The team had to persuade the local farmers to commercialize the production of subsistence crop therefore enabling them to squeeze out more money from their farming efforts. In terms of the science, increasing productivity per hectare, Elizabeth and her team had done a fairly good job. The team also did quite well in terms of developing viable alternative commercial models for the farmers. But then the most significant challenge was the fact that the farmers were unable to attract premium prices for their products.

"The farmers would produce the crops using the highest standards, but then they could not attract the commensurate prices. In a good number of cases, it meant that they were barely breaking even. It was not really worth it for the small-scale farmers."

The onus then fell to Elizabeth to persuade the team to slightly adjust their approach. Because it was a global project that was funded by a commercial venture with half the team based in Europe. It was a frustrating exercise, and Elizabeth might as well have been trying to push a boulder up a hill. Persuading the team that this was Africa and that they would need a lot more time and patience was an unpopular position to advance, and a fundamental cause of disagreement between her and other team members in the project. The realities of timelines and deliverables were also difficult to communicate.

"But you can do that in just 2 business days, can't you?" one of the team members would occasionally query.

"The sites are 400 kilometres apart," Elizabeth would explain in suppressed frustration.

"Yes, but that is only 4 hours' drive," they would insist, oblivious of the fact that the driving conditions in rural Kenya meant nearly a night and day difference as compared to Europe, and that one would need much more than 4 hours. In fact, Elizabeth would normally require up to 6 hours driving between two project sites, and the groundwork would involve more than just driving or showing up at the site. She would also need to talk to the farmers, retailers and government officials, build trust and communication channels with them and persuade them to come test the new approach the company was promoting.

"You couldn't just walk in there and start giving them instructions and advice. They would look at you blankly and wonder what a young city girl was doing in the country, showing up in a huge off-road 4X4 and giving them instructions on how to run their businesses."

Therefore, making her colleagues who were not based in Kenya, and a number of whom had never had an experience of Africa, understand business in Africa became a significant challenge for her. It was as if her whole job description had been redefined overnight. Teaching them that there is a certain way things are done in Africa–and specifically in Kenya–became increasingly difficult. So much so that her effectiveness and ability to execute her role was now placed on the scales. Nevertheless, this was only the first key challenge she faced.

The second was that the parameters for the project's success were more sales-oriented, and leaned largely on the organization's sales numbers rather than the farmers'. While the organization was working with farmers to improve their productivity, which should have been a key performance indicator, the organization focused on its own sales metrics. Elizabeth was a little less than riled with this approach, which to her recollection, was not apparent or explicitly shared before she signed up. She learned with a jolt that the targets had become how much of the chemicals, seeds, and other inputs the organization could sell to the farmers.

"These metrics did not correlate, and from a cursory analysis it appeared we had somewhat lopsided goals to pursue. I suddenly felt like we were on the same road but traveling different lanes and that the lanes were just about to split into different directions. Soon enough, we were butting heads about our own sales numbers."

Fully convinced that she no longer shared the same values with the organization, Elizabeth finally left. Barely 6 months later, she received word that the project had collapsed in its entirety. The queer and almost maniacal focus on its own sales targets had virtually cut off the limbs of the project and its ability to realize its original, core aims. Looking back on the project, Elizabeth couldn't help thinking that, had the organization been patient for 2 more years, they would now be reaping enormous benefits and be positioned, most likely, as the market leaders in their product category. The organization wanted to have everything in a hurry, 6 to 9 months in some instances, and she knew that it would not work like that in Kenya.

Elizabeth believes that she diligently made her contribution through her role to help deliver all the key elements of the project, which, in many ways, were a milestone in their own right. She had been heavily involved in implementing and setting up the project's foundational elements. The project had trained the farmers on the kinds of seeds to use, the spray programs, irrigation techniques, and even created a technology leveraged peer training system for the farmers who were not part of the pilot program. However, and to her utter consternation, pressure to deliver sales numbers began piling up.

"Since I was not looking so much to deliver sales numbers as I was focusing on improving the farmers' production capacity, it was a cue for me to pack up and leave. We no longer had a shared vision."

On the Importance of Networking

One of Elizabeth's earliest assignments, back in 2010 when she closed down her business, was the development of an alumni network for the German Development Cooperation Agencies. One of the key requirements for the job was being able to talk to people, network with people, enable them to network, organize and facilitate events where they had the possibility to develop and implement a range of projects. The immediate side effect of this job was that her Rolodex grew several times larger, almost overnight. This, she reminisces, allowed for access to more information, helpful advice, and connections that helped set up her consultancy practice.

The development community understands Elizabeth's role and the value she brings, and are willing to pay for it. However, the demand is foreign agency driven and the beneficiaries–governments and regional bodies–only ever ask for such services if the donors are going to pay.

"There is a need for my services when organizations engage in projects that involve a number of stakeholders, be they governments or regional economic bodies. Strangely, these bodies hardly demand the kind of services that I provide despite the fact that they need them most."

Interestingly, the private sector does not understand Elizabeth's role or even why they need her. Therefore, they would easily pay a Harvard PhD strategy expert about $160,000 to write a strategy or business plan, but they would not pay someone like Elizabeth even a fraction of that amount to go and facilitate the sessions. In the end, they will likely not get the desired results in terms of execution, and they will struggle to pinpoint the disconnect. But Elizabeth sees it clearly.

"On the one hand, you have a guy who is a brilliant strategy development expert, but on the other, you have someone who does not understand people and processes. He or she may not understand how to adapt the strategy to the capacity of the organization and its operational context. You have to undertake a participatory approach so that everyone can own the strategy. Only then will every employee want to play a part."

The idea, Elizabeth believes, is not so much to pay a consultant to write a strategy as much as bringing in the whole team to develop a strategy that they will be self-driven to implement.

Word of Advice

Elizabeth speaks quite fondly of Rudyard Kipling's poem "If," despite the fact that the ending may feel a little gender-insensitive. Of course, I had heard of Rudyard Kipling before, but I was not aware that this is one of his most famous poems. Since I looked it up upon Elizabeth's recommendation, the poem has lodged itself into my subconscious. For days, my mind ruminated on the few lines that Elizabeth had shared with me during the interview, particularly the ending. It was crystal clear why the poem resonates with her and her experiences through her life and entrepreneurial journey. Here are the last four lines of the poem:

If you can fill the unforgiving minute

With sixty seconds' worth of distance run,

Yours is the Earth and everything that's in it,

And—which is more—you'll be a Man, my son!

The underlying wisdom is generally applicable, as Kipling's poem fits perfectly well to Elizabeth's experience, with a minor correction to its ending: "You'll be a Woman, my daughter!"

When I first asked about her experience as a woman entrepreneur in Africa, she swiftly cut me off mid-sentence. "I don't really experience myself as a woman entrepreneur. I believe we are all just entrepreneurs, and we experience the same set of challenges," she chimed unreservedly.

Looking back and reflecting on her experiences and journey thus far, Elizabeth insists that Rudyard Kipling's poem "If" rings true for nearly every stage of her journey. There will always be success and failures, ups and downs, including all manners of challenges. This might sound like one of the oldest pieces of wisdom or advice, but it is no less true, and is still applicable to any set of circumstances. There will be both happy and sad moments. But if you can handle all these things, hang on, and keep moving and improving, then, as the poem concludes, "You will be a man, my son."

"Every path has its own set of challenges, and I do not think that it would have been any easier if I had taken any other path," she avers.

Elizabeth's advice to anyone intending to follow the consultancy path is that one should never select assignments based on the amount of money they pay, but rather on the experience and the amount of learning you will get. This, she believes, is particularly critical at the early stages. However, even at this later stage of her career, Elizabeth still picks her assignments based on what she is going to learn. She notes that sometimes there's nowhere else to get these vital lessons other than from actual experience. Therefore, you'll have to carefully pick your assignments with this in mind.

"Whenever I have to choose between two assignments, one of which I can do in my sleep, while the other would require me to be creative or stretch to a target, I'd most probably take the latter. I would most likely take one in which I would learn new things, experience different systems, countries, and cultures."

Elizabeth lives in Nairobi, Kenya, with her husband and son. She mostly works within Nairobi but also moves around the world from time to time to wherever she is required to do her work. Most of her clients at the moment are development agencies.

She has never once practiced architecture.

Takeaway:

- Consider investing time and efforts into building a solid and balanced network of people and mentors who can provide valuable advice and business leads.
- In tackling competition from international firms, leverage knowledge of domestic issues and local expertise.

Chapter XVII

Development Is the Sum of Individual Developments

The writing on the certificate reads: *Reconnaissance du BIT: Prix 2016.* A second line, just above the name, mentions PRIX DU LEADERSHIP. The calligrapher had put much effort into scripting the name, *Christian Ntsay,* with much artistry. His first name was actually Louis, but for some reason, everybody he knew, with the exception of his siblings, called him by his middle name, Christian.

It was April 4, 2016, and although it was still early spring in Geneva, with temperatures reluctant to rise after the cold winter, Christian could not help but feel the unmistakable warmth of pride running at high speed in his veins. Nobody saw it, but he shed a tear that he was unable to hold back. A single tear as he held onto this award that he squeezed ever tighter to his chest. He could not in any case afford to show more emotions, as the Director General of ILO was standing next to him in the boardroom, showering him with congratulatory remarks and firmly shaking his hand in front of a room filled with senior officials from the organization.

Straight-Shooting over a Dinner at "Chez Loutcha"

In June 2017, while on a business trip to West Africa, I met with an old acquaintance of mine in Dakar, Senegal, Professor of Endocrinology Naby Baldé from Guinea, Conakry. Naby is the highest authority in sub-Saharan Africa on diabetes in children. A well-educated and soft-spoken Peulh from Labé in Guinea, Naby is a real delight to spend an evening with deconstructing the world. We were sharing a *Thieboudienne* at Chez Loutcha, a Cape Verde restaurant in Rue Mousse Diop in Dakar.[1] Naby asked me about the projects I was working on. Naby had eaten at Chez Loutcha the day before and loved the food, so he suggested we have dinner at the restaurant, as it was not far from the Pullman Téranga, the hotel we were both staying at.

Chez Loutcha was not the typical posh restaurant, but even for a person generally indifferent to food as I am, the food was seriously good and tasty. I went on discussing my job at work and, one thing leading to another, the book I had started several months ago on *Doing Business in Africa*. I enthusiastically elaborated on specifics about each of the

---

[1] West African dish made of rice, fish, and tomato sauce originally from Senegal. Thieboudienne means "rice with fish" in Wolof, a language spoken in Senegal, Gambia, and Mauritania. The dish has different names in Guinea and Côte d'Ivoire (Riz au gras) and in Ghana and Nigeria (Jollof rice) where it's one of the most popular dishes

articles and contributions, and on my satisfaction to have completed the manuscript that I was about to publish.

"Your project seems intent on focusing on people from the private sector," he said as he took some of the fish. He was highlighting the stance that I had deliberately decided on when starting the project. The reasons were simple. For one, all the people I knew well were from the private sector, and, second, civil servants in the public sector in Africa are too often given a bad name in Africa.

"I understand where you're coming from, Ben, and that's totally legitimate as you are a business person, in essence," he continued. "The only issue is, regardless of your reasons, you cannot discard the perspective of the public sector—the politicians, that is to say. Listen, these are the policymakers who are responsible for setting up the very rules of engagement your businesspeople evolve in. I think it might be interesting to also hear from them."

Naby had a point. I had known it all along, but only needed someone to tell it to my face. Naby was still the straightforward man I knew. Shooting at point-blank range. That was refreshing, very refreshing.

Christian Ntsay

Christian had been minister of tourism in his native Madagascar from 2002 to 2003. We were put in contact by a mutual friend who knew what I was looking for in terms of profile with experience in the public sector. Christian perfectly fit the bill, and I was thrilled with the idea that he wanted to join our bandwagon and share his experience as a minister in charge of bringing tourism investments to his country and making the place more attractive for tourists.

"I am an economist by training. In terms of education, I completed my Master's degree at the University in Tana in 1984 before going to CEFEB Paris and Marseille for a DEA in economics.[1,2] After university in Marseille, I worked as a junior auditor at a shipyard in Marseille, which at the time was one of the best shipyards in the world. I came back to Madagascar in 1986 and worked for various state-owned companies. I joined another shipyard, the Société d'Études, de Construction et de Réparation Navales (Secren S.A.) in Diego Suarez, Antsiranana, in the north of the country. I took the position of administrative and financial director, deputy director general, and later on the

---

[1] Short for Antananarivo, Capital of Madagascar

[2] Diplôme d'Etudes Approfondies

position of director general. I subsequently moved to Solima, the state-owned oil company where I was director general until 1997. I also held positions as Chairman of the board of two tourism companies at the time. In 2002, I was appointed minister of tourism, a position that I had for two years."

In 2001, Madagascar was emerging from a major political crisis that lasted several months and considerably dented its economy. New ideas were urgently needed to boost the economy, especially in sectors such as tourism, which accounts for about 6 percent of its GDP and employs over 200,000 people.

"We received about 350,000 tourists a year in Madagascar before the crisis," Christian recalls. "This number plunged to 85,000 after the crisis."

Madagascar is an island with superb beaches and a unique biodiversity. Besides being the number one exporter of vanilla in the world, some of the world's most amazing wildlife—such as the panther chameleon, the blue coua, the tomato frog, the cat-like lemurs sifaka and indri, or the Madagascar pochard—can only be found in Madagascar.

Facing Headwinds from the Start

"From a business standpoint, Madagascar, like many

other African countries, is a small market," Christian says. "And in order to get an edge or even survive, some operators try to get closer to the world of politics. They are on the lookout for opportunities. The situation creates unnatural relationships and cross-links where the worlds of business and politics gets intertwined, which is not necessarily beneficial to the general public in the end."

Christian then recounts a specific instance, a World Tourism Fair where several local tour operators fought to be included in the official delegation from Madagascar. He was fairly surprised to see how some operators were ready to go to great lengths to join the delegation, and try to influence the decision by contacting other members of the government to have their way. This experience left a vivid impression on Christian. He was far from being a novice in politics, having for a long time managed state-owned companies, but the intensity of the strong headwinds he faced from some of the private operators to steer his department in the direction he felt was best for his country was somewhat new to him.

In Africa, more than in other parts of the world, Christian believes, the need for stronger laws and better discipline in following the rule of law is critical to advance business and private enterprise. He sees this as a zero-sum game, in which political power and intervention need to be drawn to the minimal, in order to have transparent market forces that may play a higher role. I once met President Thabo Mbeki at a business lunch in Madrid. The man who had the illustrious task of succeeding President Nelson Mandela at the helm of the Republic of South Africa told me: "You know Ben, overall, we do not have a policy issue in Africa. We have however a policy implementation issue in the continent".

Maison du Tourisme

A project that Christian was keen on reinvigorating during his tenure as minister of tourism was the concept of Maison du Tourisme, which was a unit at the ministry responsible for promoting Madagascar as a must-see tourist destination. Maison du Tourisme was financed by funds raised via hotels, from the guests' payment of a vignette fee. The mechanism was not working smoothly, and payments were either not collected or simply not transferred to the government. Hotel operators complained that the benefits of the system were not tangible enough for them to oversee and that they could not understand why they should engage in the extra work, especially as it made their room rates less attractive. In order to improve the collection of the vignette fee and invest in increasing tourists' interest in Madagascar, Christian created the National Office of Tourism and regional offices of tourism, which were then closer to the hotels and could support them better on a day-to-day basis. Once again, the opportunity for an investment from the government attracted an interest from the private sector, from people with a connection in political circles, as they wanted to benefit more than their competition from the government's efforts.

"From a general perspective, economic development in Africa is largely supported by public investments, so governments play a major role in the private sector's prosperity. So the bigger the role a government plays, the tighter are the links the private sector tries to create with the government. This is a complex issue. There is a need to find ways to reduce the role the government plays over the long run, as this becomes a matter of survival for the private sector in our countries."

The Most Important Help for Business in Africa

Education is, according to Christian, the most important investment Africa could ever make to steer itself onto greener pastures. Not only for the sake of the private enterprise, but for the sake of societies as a whole. One out of three Malagasy are illiterate, and this

ratio can be as high as two out of three in some African countries. Christian considers the proportion of illiteracy in a country to be echoed in the various social groups in society. A third of illiterate globally in Madagascar translates, as he puts it, into a third of construction workers, a third of farmers, a third of politicians, etc. are illiterate. Christian is being deliberately provocative, as he knows that the distribution of the population on illiteracy tends to have much larger proportions in rural and economically underprivileged groups of the population, but his point is clear: The more educated a population is, the better they can contribute to advancing the development agenda of their country.

"You know, Ben, I have always believed that development was the sum of self-developments we achieve at the individual level. We become developed as nations when we manage for each person to achieve progress at the individual level. And this is the promise that better education delivers—individual development."

Takeaway:

- Africa needs a stronger judicial platform and the discipline for all to abide by the rule of law in order for businesses to make the most of the policies drafted to support economic development.
- Making the most of policies to advance business agendas can support.

Contributors

Many thanks to

Abdoulaye Wann – Founder of Hamdallaye Schools, Conakry—Guinea

John Sargeant – Founder and Managing Partner, BroadReach Healthcare, Cape Town—South Africa

Ernest Darkwo – Founder and Managing Partner, BroadReach Healthcare, Cape Town—South Africa

Ruka Sanusi – Management Consultant, Founder and Principal of Alldens Lane, Accra— Ghana

Aboubakar Coulibaly – Managing Partner, Lithium Africa Consulting, Abidjan—Côte d'Ivoire

Sunil Gupte – Group Managing Director for the Fareast Mercantile Group, Dubai—United Arab Emirates

Feyi Olobodun – Managing Director/CEO, Insight Publicis Nigeria, Lagos—Nigeria

Daniel Ntim-Addae – Architect, MBA, CEO at BrightStone Capital Ghana Ltd, Accra, Ghana

R. Ananth Narayan – Retired, former Managing Director, WorldWide Commercial Ventures, Lagos—Nigeria

Patrick Mennesson – Pharmacist, Administrator/Executive

Director General, La Grande Pharmacie des Forestiers, Libreville—Gabon

Mohamed Eldawi – MBA, Supply Chain Expert, Khartoum—Sudan

Adama Ballo – Ingénieur Commercial, Founder, and Managing Director, Harmonies, Abidjan — Côte d'Ivoire

Elikem Nutifafa Kuenyehia – Lawyer, MBA Chairman, ENSafrica Ghana, Accra, Ghana

Prosper Tchouambé – MBA, General Manager at Trans-Resources Africa, Abidjan, Côte d'Ivoire

François Soma – Ingénieur HEC Lausanne, Founder, and Managing Director, BSI Import-Export SARL, Bussigny-près-Lausanne — Switzerland

Elizabeth S. Maloba – Consultant, Entrepreneur and Business Growth Facilitator, Nairobi — Kenya

Christian Ntsay – Economist, Former Tourism Minister of the Republic of Madagascar, ILO Director for Indian Ocean, Antananarivo — Madagascar

for your invaluable assistance in the project. I am very grateful for your help and contribution.

Special thanks to John Nasaye Owuor in Nairobi.